The Heart of Anger

Practical Help for the Prevention and Cure of Anger in Children

Lou Priolo

Foreword by John MacArthur, Jr.

The Heart of Anger

Calvary Press Publishing

www.calvarypress.com / 1-800-247-6553

Calvary Press

2005 Merrick Rd. #341

Merrick, NY. 11566

1-800-247-6553

ISBN 978-1-879737-28-0

Book and Cover Design by Michael Rotolo

This work was originally published with the title of *How to Help Angry Kids* 1996

Unless otherwise noted, the Bible quotations contained in this book are from the New American Standard Bible, ©by the Lockman Foundation 1960, 1962, 1963, 1968, 1971, 1972, 1973, 1975, 1977. Used by permission. Bible verses marked KJV were taken from the King James Version; those marked NKJV were taken from the New King James Version; those marked NIV were taken from the New International Version.

Priolo, Louis Paul, 1954–
    The Heart of Anger
Recommended Dewey Decimal Classification: 234
Suggested Subject Headings:
    1. Christian Living—anger—counseling literature
    2. Religion—Christian literature—counseling literature
    3. The Bible—anger—teaching literature.
    I. Title

Calvary Press Publishing is a Not-For-Profit Ministry of the Grace Reformed Baptist Church of Long Island, New York. We are dedicated to publishing literature which communicates the biblical doctrines of the Sovereignty of God and God's Grace in the saving of mankind. These truths have historically been best articulated in the theology which resulted as a consequence of the Protestant Reformation of the Sixteenth Century. This theology which has come to be known as Reformed Theology is what we are particularly desirous of seeing put into print whenever there is a vacancy of such material in the Christian book marketplace. Also read our Mission Statement at the back of this book.

Manufactured in the United States of America

To Sophia

"A Child who loves wisdom makes his father glad"
Proverbs 29:3

I pray that you may be filled with the knowledge of His will in all spiritual wisdom and understanding, so that you may live a life worthy of the Lord and that you may please Him in every way; may you bear fruit in every good work as you grow in the knowledge of God.

Lou Priolo is the Director of the Christian Counseling Institute of Atlanta, Georgia. He is a graduate of Calvary Bible College and Liberty University. Lou has been a full time biblical counselor and instructor for over twelve years and is a Fellow of the National Association of Nouthetic Counselors. Lou has been blessed to share his life with his wife Kim and his daughter Sophia.

Contents

Acknowledgements

I shall not be able to acknowledge, until glory, all those individuals who have been used by God to influence my life and ministry. It is certain that I could never remember them all or recognize all of those to whom, in many ways still unknown to me, I am indebted and should be thankful. Some of them (whose books have influenced me) have gone to glory before I was born; others I have lost contact with and may not see again until then.

Here are those whose direct assistance in the publication of this book has been greatly appreciated—

Susan Fitzgerrald who was the first to chip away the rough edges of the initial draft;

John Sowell whose work on the first six chapters is appreciated more than he will ever know;

Kim Priolo who typed, retyped and then typed again every revision in the tedious process of refining this work;

Jay Adams who put the first coat of polish on the manuscript and wrote such an enthusastic preface;

David Powlison who put polish on the polish; and finally Jan Haley and Barbara Lerch for their ideas on how to make this resource more user friendly.

Foreword

Lou Priolo has a remarkable gift for taking truths that many parents find difficult and elusive, and unfolding them with incredible clarity and simplicity. You might say he cuts through the Gordian Knot of biblical parenting. He wields the sword of the Spirit in a creative way, unravelling some difficult parenting problems that seem impossibly puzzling to many. And he reveals that raising children in a biblical manner does not have to be as hard as most people make it.

The Heart of Anger is help for parents of angry children. It goes beyond the external manifestations of anger, and shows how to deal with the internal source of anger— the thoughts and motives of the heart (Heb. 4:12). The book will also be helpful to parents who themselves struggle with sinful anger.

I know of no other work that addresses this problem with such practical, applicable biblical wisdom— and without the shallow pop psychology that is so prevalent in many parenting books. This wonderful book will encourage struggling parents— even those whose children do *not* struggle with anger— and it will help fortify families against the onslaughts of an evil, angry age.

—John MacArthur

Preface

Lou Priolo has written an eminently readable, practical book about a problem frequently encountered but rarely addressed. It is a book whose time has come. And he has done so basing his work on biblical principles and practices. Every nouthetic counselor will want his own copy as well as some to give away or lend. Pastors will put it in their libraries and church bookstores. Parents will devour it. Christian children will benefit from it, and the Church in general will be in Lou's debt for writing it. Liberals will loathe it and psychologists will "pooh-pooh" it. There is nothing else like it; I expect it to do much good.

Lou, let me be the first to thank you for allowing me the opportunity to read the book in its manuscript form. I congratulate you on your efforts for Him! This book was needed.

—Jay E. Adams

A Word from the Author

This was not the first book I wanted to write. There are at least half a dozen other issues with which I would have preferred to break into the book writing arena. Providentially though, the Lord directed the course of events so that the material contained in this work was developed and tested more quickly than I could have anticipated. Whenever this material has been presented in counseling courses, seminars, and lectures, its success has been tremendous. The response of people and their evident hunger for help and guidance in these matters has been overwhelming. Furthermore, requests for this helpful material to be published has outnumbered requests for other material two to one. For these reasons this book was given top priority.

The Heart of Anger contains some rather newly developed applications of the timeless wisdom revealed in God's Word. This is in contrast to the plethora of so-called *"Christian"* books on child training which contain more pagan worldly psychology than exhortation from the all sufficient Holy Scripture. It was not intended to be a complete all-purpose book on parenting or an exhaustive treatment of angry children.

I suggest the book is best understood as a basic tool kit. You will find some of the more useful and readily learned tools for understanding, preventing and correcting anger in children. It will even help you to avoid provoking anger in your children that you may not have been aware you were doing. You probably won't need every one of these tools for every job (and it doesn't contain every available tool for correcting anger and other discipline problems), but once you understand the concepts and become proficient with these tools you will be much better equipped to deal in a godly manner with anger in your child's life.

I hope you will be thoroughly persuaded by its biblical and theological accuracy. Most of all, I believe this material will offer the help and real hope to parents looking for biblical solutions to anger-related childhood problems.

God Bless you — Lou Priolo

Angry Kids

Jim and Linda sat across the desk from me with tears in their eyes. They were frustrated because their ten year old son was so difficult to manage. Linda began their story:

"We can't control Joshua. He is determined to have his own way. We're embarrassed by how he talks to us. His teacher says he disrupts the whole class. She's even suggested that he may need to be placed on medication to control his behavior. We've tried disciplining him, but we gave up when he got so angry that we became frightened. I feel guilty and ashamed because I have failed as a mother. We don't know what to do, and I feel as if there is no hope. We're so afraid that if Joshua doesn't get help now, he is going to be a first class rebel in just a few years."

Jim and Linda[1], like many parents, had lost hope. They did not see God's hand in their trial. They had lost sight of their parental responsibilities as a "joint effort" with God, who promises to provide the wisdom (Jam. 1:5), instruction (2 Pet. 1:3), ability (Phil. 2:13), and desire (Phil. 2:13) to be good parents. It is the responsibility of Joshua's parents to love God and Joshua by obeying God's Word in bringing Joshua up in the "discipline and instruction of the Lord" (Eph. 6:4). Perhaps you, like Jim and Linda, have forgotten that God will not ask you as a Christian to follow any biblical mandate without providing the grace and ability to carry it out. As you read this book, you will find hope in God's provisions which will enable you to bring up your children "in the discipline and instruction of the Lord" (Eph. 6:4).

The Heart of Anger

An Unusual Policy

As Jim and Linda proceeded with their story, they were still wondering why our counseling center has a rather unusual policy regarding the counseling of children. As a rule, unless a crisis or an emergency exists, we will not see a child by himself without first having two or three sessions with the parents. As I explained to Jim and Linda, the reason for this policy is not to allow them to gossip about or slander their son to me. Neither is it to give them the opportunity to predispose me against him. Rather the purpose of this policy is to identify how Jim and Linda may be sinning against Josh so that I may help them remove the beam from their own eyes before they attempt to help Josh remove the splinter from his.[2]

Jim and Linda continued providing data in answer to specific questions which have been designed to help us formulate a tentative diagnosis of the existing problems within their family. While the process of data collection and diagnosis went on, I listened for patterns of behavior that could be identified as pathological from a biblical point of view, "not in words taught by human wisdom, but in those taught by the Spirit, combining spiritual (thoughts) with spiritual (words)" (1 Cor. 2:13). In other words, I was trying to understand Josh's problem from God's point of view using biblical terminology to make the diagnosis.

After some time, I walked over to the white board in my office. I then began listing the patterns of behavior I had identified in Joshua. Based on his parents' observations, I identified eleven undesirable behavior patterns:

- *Outbursts of anger / temper tantrums*
- *Argumentation / quarrelsome debates*
- *Disrespect*
- *Fighting / violence*
- *Animosity*

- *Cruelty .*
- *Strife / antagonism*
- *Acts of vengeance*
- *Malice*
- *Bitterness*
- *Discouragement / apathy, indifference*

"Can you see a common denominator in all of these behaviors?" I asked.

"Yes! I never thought of it like that before," Linda said, "It's anger! Joshua has an anger problem."

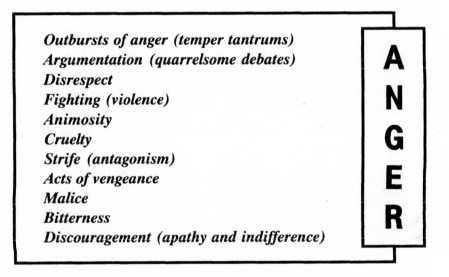

Outbursts of anger (temper tantrums)
Argumentation (quarrelsome debates)
Disrespect
Fighting (violence)
Animosity
Cruelty
Strife (antagonism)
Acts of vengeance
Malice
Bitterness
Discouragement (apathy and indifference)

A N G E R

Completing the diagram, I explained, "It looks as though Joshua may have developed some of the characteristics of the angry man described in Proverbs.

"An angry man stirs up strife, And a hot-tempered man abounds in transgression" (Prov. 29:22).

"Do not associate with a man given to anger; Or go with a hot-tempered man, Lest you learn his ways, And find a snare for yourself" (Prov. 22:24-25).

Characterological Sin

Q. What happens to a person who continually yields the members of his body to a particular sin?
A. He becomes a slave to the sin by which he chose to be mastered. (Rom. 6:16)

Q. What does God call an individual who continually gives himself over to folly?
A. God calls him a fool. (Prov. 26:11)

Q. How does Scripture classify someone who continually gives himself over to drunkenness?
A. Scripture classifies him as a drunkard. (1 Cor. 8:11)

Q. What is the biblical name for a person who habitually lies?
A. The biblical name for a person who habitually lies is a liar. (Prov. 17:4)

According to Scripture, when an individual continually gives himself over to a particular sin, he eventually becomes bound by that sin (Romans 6:16; John 8:34; 2 Peter 2:19). At some point in this bondage process, as he is training his heart in covetous practices (2 Peter 2:14), as the effects of his sin begin to bleed over into other areas of his life (work, family, church, and health for example), as his life becomes increasingly dominated by the characteristics and consequences of his sin (Gal. 6:7,8; Jam. 1:8), God classifies that person by the name of the sin that he allows to master him.[3] Josh is becoming "an angry man."

A part of my task as a counselor is to identify my counselee's particular bondage and then help him discover biblical alternatives to the sin he is trying to remove from his life. In Joshua's case, sinful anger was becoming a dominant characteristic of his personality. Therefore, Jim, Linda, and I, by God's grace, needed to determine the source of Joshua's anger and to find the resources to help him overcome his anger problem. Unless Josh solves his problem, it could lead to other problems, such as full-fledged rebellion.

The Developement of Rebellion

Joshua's parents, you will remember, were concerned that if his current problems were not brought under control he would rebel when he got older. Their concerns about more serious, escalating rebellion are not unfounded. Anger, especially in children, can lead to rebellion. Sinful anger is always an expression of rebellion against God and Josh is already rebelling. There is a process involving anger that leads to rebellion against authority. This process develops not just in children, but in wives who rebel against their husbands, in husbands who rebel against Christ's call to love their wives as He loved the Church, in employees who rebel against their employers, in employers who rebel against the Lord's call to kindness, in church members who rebel against the authority of the church, in church leaders who rebel against God's call to loving service and in anyone who sinfully rebels against a divinely appointed authority and against the God who is Master of all.

This anger to rebellion process often can be traced through five distinct steps. These five steps on the stairway to destruction are hurt, bitterness, anger, stubbornness, and finally rebellion:

A Wounded spirit (or feeling hurt) Proverbs 18:14 states, "A wounded spirit who can bear?" The first step in this stairway to destruction often is a sense of hurt that is spawned by an offense, whether real or perceived. Parents do something (usually involving sin, but not necessarily) to the child whose mental and emotional response produces hurt. This hurt is the seed that germinates and grows into a root of bitterness (Heb. 12:15).

Bitterness is the second step on the stairway. If the child does not respond biblically to the hurt (this would involve either forgiving the sin (Lk. 17:3), "overlooking" the sin (Prov. 19:11,

1 Pet. 4:8), or realizing that the "offense" was not wrong), he will begin to rehearse the offense in his mind, reviewing it over and over again. This practice of continually reviewing and imputing the offense not only violates 1 Corinthians 13:5 (love does not keep a running account of evil), but also cultivates the seed of hurt that matures into a "root of bitterness" (Heb. 12:15). Consequently, this root of bitterness may defile others in the family. [4]

Anger is the third step. This is the kind of anger about which the Bible warns fathers not to provoke their children. Such anger is not simply a momentary explosion that quickly dies down. Rather, it is characterological anger which was explained earlier. This is anger that has become so habitual that it becomes characteristic of the child's personality "Do not associate with a man (given) to anger; Or go with a hot-tempered man, Lest you learn his ways, And find a snare for yourself" (Prov. 22:24,25). You as a parent, of course, cannot disassociate with your angry child, but this verse may serve as a reminder of just one of the biblical consequences which result from characterological anger. Such is the anger that this book has been written to prevent and correct.

Stubbornness (insubordination) is the fourth step. "Rebellion is as the sin of witchcraft and stubbornness is as iniquity and idolatry" 1 Sam. 15:23. This step immediately precedes full-blown rebellion. The picture of stubbornness here is that of a backsliding heifer pushing her front hooves into the ground to counteract her master who is trying to push or pull her forward. The self-sufficient rebel in the making is guilty of idolatry because he believes he has become the ruler of his own destiny.

Rebellion is the final step in the decline. A rebellious child is a child whose characteristics have gone beyond that of an angry man and have assumed the characteristics of the proverbial fool. As you are reading this book, you will possibly discover that you are associated with someone who is in this final stage of rebellion. Read through the following list of characteristics of a fool and see how many of them your "rebel" has. When you are finished you may be surprised to see that the characteristics of a fool are essentially the same as those of a rebel.

25 Characteristics of a Fool

Characteristic	Proverb
Despises wisdom and instruction	*1:7*
Hates knowledge	*1:22*
Grieves his mother	*10:1*
Enjoys devising mischief	*10:23*
Right in his own eyes	*12:15*
Quick to anger	*12:16*
Hates to depart from evil	*13:19*
Deceitful	*14:8*
Arrogant and careless	*14:16*
Rejects his father's instruction	*15:5*
Despises his mother (and/or father)	*15:20*
Does not respond well to discipline	*17:10*
Does not understand wisdom	*17:16*
Has a worldly focus (a carnal value system)	*17:24*
Grieves his parents	*17:25*
Hurts his parents	*17:25*
Will not discuss any viewpoint but his own	*18:2*
Provokes others to strife and anger by his words	*18:6*
A smart mouth usually gets him into trouble	*18:7*
Is quarrelsome (contentious)	*20:3*
Is a spendthrift	*21:20*
Repeats his folly (foolishness)	*26:11*
Trusts in his own heart	*28:26*
Cannot resolve conflicts	*29:9*
Gives full vent to his anger	*29:11*

Although it is beyond the scope of this book to develop and address all the ins and outs of rebellion, two points should be made. First, the best way to deal with rebellion is to prevent it: *"A prudent man sees the evil and hides himself" (Prov. 22:3).* Second, the best insurance against the development of char-

23

acterological rebellion is the prevention of characterological anger: *"Do not be eager in your heart to be angry for anger resides in the bosom of fools" (Eccl. 7:9)*.

The Child-Centered Home

The next set of diagrams I drew for Jim and Linda pinpointed what was at the heart of Joshua's anger.

"I'm going to draw a model of two drastically different families. When I'm through, I would like for you to tell me which of the two models best represents your family. The first family revolves around the children. It is a child-centered home. [5] A child-centered home is one in which a child believes and is allowed to behave as though the entire household, parents, siblings, and even pets exist for one purpose— to please him."

A child-centered home is one in which children are allowed to commit the following indiscretions:

▷ *Interrupt adults when they are talking*
▷ *Use manipulation and rebellion to get their way*
▷ *Dictate family schedule (including meal times, bedtimes, etc.)*
▷ *Take precedence over the needs of the spouse*
▷ *Have an equal or overriding vote in all decision making matters*
▷ *Demand excessive time and attention from parents to the detriment of the other biblical responsibilities of the parents*
▷ *Escape the consequences of their sinful and irresponsible behavior*
▷ *Speak to parents as though they were peers*
▷ *Be the dominant influence in the home*
▷ *Be entertained and coddled (rather than disciplined) out of a bad mood.*

Figure 1. The Child-Centered Home

A child who is at the center of a child-centered home believes that he and his desires should be the focal point of the entire household. It is in the context of a child-centered home that many children grow up believing that society owes them a living.

The God-Centered Home

"On the other hand," I told Jim and Linda, "a God-centered home is a home that is patterned after Genesis 2:24. 'For this cause (marriage) shall a man leave his father and his mother, and shall cleave to his wife; and they shall become one flesh.' This verse is perhaps the most important specific verse on the family in the Bible. It is repeated three additional times in Scripture. It is also the least often followed. Virtually all marriage and family problems can be traced back to a failure to leave one's parents, cleave to one's spouse, or become one flesh with one's spouse."

When two people leave their respective homes to establish a new home for Christ, they become a family before any children arrive. When children are added, Mother and Father become the heads of a new decision-making unit. This unit is not a democracy. The husband is the head of this unit and the wife is his helper. The two are one flesh.

As children are born, they are welcomed into the family, but not as a part of the decision-making unit. In other words, they are part of the family, but they are not one flesh with the parents.

According to Scripture, the relationship between husband and wife is a permanent relationship which is not to be broken (Matt. 19:3-6). The authority / submission relationship between parents and their children is a temporary one which eventually is to be broken according to Genesis 2:24. One day the children will also leave home. Therefore, the relationship between a husband and wife is the priority relationship. The relationships between parents and children and between siblings are important but secondary.

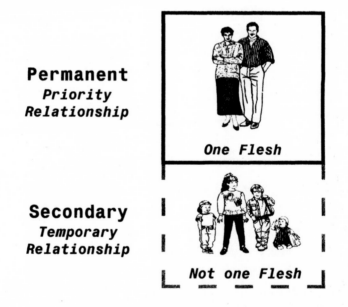

Permanent
Priority
Relationship

One Flesh

Secondary
Temporary
Relationship

Not one Flesh

Figure 2. The God-Centered Home

The concept of a God-centered home is derived from the biblical principle that the purpose of every Christian is to glorify God (1 Cor. 10:31; 1 Cor. 6:20). In contrast to a child-centered home, where pleasing and serving the child is the dominant theme, the

God-centered home is one in which everyone is committed to pleasing and serving God. God's desires are exalted over everyone else's. Everyone in the family may be expected to sacrifice personal pleasures if God's will requires it. This philosophy teaches children to serve rather than be served, to honor rather than be honored, to give (be loving) rather than take (be selfish). In God-centered homes, children are taught the following (among many others):

- *To joyfully serve others*
- *To cheerfully obey parents the first time*
- *To not interrupt parents who are speaking to each other*
- *To understand they will not always get their own way*
- *To work their schedule around their parents' schedule*
- *To have input into family decisions but not necessarily an equal vote*
- *To understand that God has given their parents other responsibilities in addition to meeting their needs*
- *To suffer the natural consequences of their sinful and irresponsible behavior*
- *To not speak to parents as though they were peers but honor them as spiritual authorities*
- *To esteem others as more important than themselves*
- *To fulfill various household responsibilities (chores)*
- *To protect themselves from certain bad influences*
- *To not divide parents over disciplinary issues*
- *To not be more intimate with either parent than the parents are with each other*

After these two models were explained to Jim and Linda, I asked them to identify the pattern that best described their home most often. They chose the child-centered home. So have the overwhelming majority of parents of angry children I've asked over the years.

Jim, Linda and Joshua are not alone. How about you? Which model best describes your household: the child-centered or the God-centered home?

Child-Centered	God-Centered
The child perceives that the entire family exists essentially to please and make him or her happy. Mother and Father and siblings exist only to serve and meet the child's needs and desires.	*The child perceives that the husband is the head of the family and the wife is submissive to her husband. Theirs is the primary relationship. It is permanent and exists to glorify God. Children have a secondary and temporary relationship.*

Figure 3. The Child-Centered vs. The God-Centered Home

As the counseling process continues each family member must understand and implement the biblical principles needed to move from a child-centered to a God-centered home. As a result of such implementation, tension, unresolved conflicts, frustration, and despair can gradually be replaced by harmony, conflict resolution, peace, and hope. Jesus Christ is the loving Redeemer of sinners, the Good Shepherd of the wandering, the Great Physician of the needy.

If your home, like so many in our day, is patterned more closely after the child-centered model than the God-centered model, the biblical principles explained in the following chapters can equip you to make the transition from a home where chaos rules to a home where the peace of Christ rules.

In this chapter we've identified two major issues associated with angry children: characterological anger and child-oriented homes. In the next, we'll discuss what you may be doing to contribute to your child's anger problem.

Provocative Parents

I had tentatively diagnosed Joshua as possessing characterological anger. He qualified, in other words, for the dubious distinction of being an angry man. I asked Jim and Linda another question. "Can you think of a verse in the Bible that talks about angry children?"

"Yes, 'Fathers, do not provoke your children to anger,'" Jim said, as the expression on his face changed from confidence that he knew the right answer, to dismay that he and Linda might somehow be culpable of provoking Joshua.

"That's right", I explained, "Ephesians 6:4 says that rather than provoking your children, you should bring them up in the discipline and instruction of the Lord. In a parallel passage, Colossians 3:21, Paul uses a different word to express the same idea, 'Fathers, do not exasperate your children, that they may not lose heart (or be discouraged).'"

Who's To Blame?

At this point, I had to remind Jim and Linda that I was not a Freudian psychologist interested in blaming them for their child's problems. "You two are big sinners. Joshua is a little sinner. As a sinner, he is 100% responsible before God for his anger problem, and must assume that responsibility. God expects him not to be sinfully angry, regardless of how his parents provoke him. God expects him to change whether you choose to or not. But the two of you are responsible before God, not to contribute to Joshua's anger problem. To the degree that you are provoking him to anger, you must stop. To whatever degree you stop provoking him, you can make it easier for Joshua to correct his anger problem. The child-centered home in which Joshua lives, a situation which you are responsible for allowing to come to pass, is likely one of a number of parental provocations that must be addressed if you truly want to help him repent from his frequent episodes of being angry."

The rest of the first counseling session (with corresponding homework assignments), as well as the next two sessions, were devoted to identifying and removing those parental provocations that were likely affecting Joshua's behavior. By the time I did have my first session with Josh, his behavior had already begun to improve even though I had spent the first three sessions counseling only his parents. There has even been a time or two in my ministry to hurting parents that counseling the child was really not necessary. This was because, in such cases, the provocations were few and the parents were willing to thoroughly restructure their lives according to biblical priorities.

Although not exhaustive, the following twenty five conditions or behaviors represent some of the most common ways that parents tend to provoke their children to anger.

25 Ways That Parents Provoke Their Children to Anger

1. Lack of Marital Harmony

"For this cause a man shall leave his father and his mother, and shall cleave to his wife; and they shall become one flesh" (Gen. 2:24).

"See to it that no one comes short of the grace of God; that no root of bitterness springing up causes trouble, and by it many be defiled" (Heb. 12:15).

Provocative Parents

Perhaps the greatest provocation of anger in children is parents who do not live with each other in the harmony that the Scriptures prescribe. The verse above, containing the term "one flesh," appears a total of five times in the Bible. If a husband and wife do not develop the "one flesh" intimacy intended by God, then over time various other problems will develop. Of these, one of the most common is that each spouse is tempted to develop a deeper level of intimacy with something or someone else, rather than with their spouse. Typically, the husband develops closer ties with people at work or play (or with the job or recreation itself). The wife, characteristically, develops a spiritually unbalanced relationship with the children. Once this occurs, it is usually just a matter of time before the home becomes child-centered.

Another correlation between lack of marital harmony and angry children is the defiling effect that bitterness has on others. As the child observes the resentment that results from his parents' lack of harmony, he becomes more susceptible to acquiring those bitter thoughts, motives, attitudes, and actions that he has seen modeled by them. Look again at Hebrews 12:15. "See to it that no one comes short of the grace of God; that no root of bitterness springing up causes trouble, and by it many be defiled." The "many" most likely to be defiled when Mom and Dad are bitter at each other are the children. Remember also, that bitterness is one of the links in the developmental chain of anger to rebellion. If you can keep your children from developing bitterness, you will have gone a long way in preventing them from developing characterological anger and rebellion.

2. Establishing and Maintaining a Child-Centered Home

"The rod and reproof give wisdom, But a child who gets his own way brings shame to his mother" (Prov. 29:15).

Allow me to make one additional point about a child-centered home. When parents do not establish a home that is clearly Christ-centered (one in which each member understands his biblical role in the family and is committed to please Christ more than self), it is likely that the home will be child-centered. If the husband and wife do not work at being closer to each other than to the child, the child may view himself as equal to, rather than as a subordinate to them. In such "democratic" households, children tend to become angry when their desires do not get placed on equal status with the desires of their parents.

3. Modeling Sinful Anger

"Do not associate with a man given to anger; or go with a hot-tempered man, lest you learn his ways, and find a snare for yourself" (Prov. 22:24,25).

Have your children been snared by learning (picking up) any of your angry ways? When you or your spouse model sinful anger, you may inadvertently teach your children that the only way to solve problems is to win. Children who regularly observe such poor examples of communication often grow up without having the necessary biblical resources with which to resolve conflicts and to solve people-problems. If you or your spouse habitually are given to inappropriate manifestations of anger, you would do well to read this book twice: once focusing on correcting your own anger problem, then focusing on helping your child correct his anger.

4. Habitually Disciplining While Angry

"O Lord, rebuke me not in Thy wrath; and chasten me not in Thy burning anger" (Ps. 38:1).

When you are angry, it is easier for you to overdiscipline. Your anger may be perceived by your child as a personal attack. If he views your discipline as such, he will likely suspect that your motive for the discipline is vindictive rather than corrective. If he concludes that this is your motive (thus violating 1 Cor. 4:5), he will find it difficult not to get angry. The emphasis of your thinking and of your subsequent discipline should be on what the child has done *by sinning against God, not on how his action has caused you some personal discomfort, trouble, or embarrassment.*

"Be angry, and yet do not sin; do not let the sun go down on your anger, and do not give the devil an opportunity" (Eph. 4:26, 27).

"Everyone must be quick to hear, slow to speak, and slow to anger; for the anger of man does not achieve the righteousness of God" (James 1:19, 20).

If you do find yourself more upset because your child has sinned against you than you are because he sinned against God, you must quickly and prayerfully get your heart in such a state that personal desires are temporarily set aside. You must be willing to lay aside your personal rights and forgive your child's offense against you so that you may focus on fulfilling your parental obligations to him. Only then can you discipline your child with the assurance that your passion is not unholy anger.

5. Scolding

"Let no unwholesome word proceed from your mouth, but only such (a word) as is good for edification according to the need (of the moment), that it may give grace to those who hear" (Eph. 4:29).

"And while He was in Bethany at the home of Simon the leper, and reclining (at the table), there came a woman with an alabaster vial of very costly perfume of pure nard; (and) she broke the vial and poured it over His head. But some were indignantly (remarking) to one another, 'Why has this perfume been wasted? For this perfume might have been sold for over three hundred denarii, and (the money) given to the poor.' And they were scolding her" (Mark 14:3-5).

One of the Greek words from which the term scolding (in the above text) was derived, means "to snort with anger." It was used to describe the snorting of horses. In his book, *Hints on Child Training* [6], first published in 1891, H. Clay Trumbull, considered by many to be the founder of Sunday school, explains:

"To 'scold' is to assail or revile with boisterous speech. The word itself seems to have a primary meaning akin to that of barking or howling.

Scolding is always an expression of a bad spirit and of a loss of temper. . . the essence of the scolding is in the multiplication of hot words in expression of strong feelings that, while eminently natural, ought to be held in better control.

If a child has done wrong, a child needs talking to; but no parent ought to talk to a child while that parent is unable to talk in a natural tone of voice, and with carefully measured words. If the parent is tempted to speak rapidly, or to multiply words without stopping to weigh them, or to show an excited state of feeling, the parent's first duty is to gain entire self-control. Until that control is secured, there is no use of the parent's trying to attempt any measure of child training. The loss of self-control is for the time being an utter loss of power for the control of others.

In giving commands or in giving censure to a child, the fewer and the more calmly spoken words the better. A child soon learns that scolding means less than quiet talking; and he even comes to find a certain satisfaction in waiting silently until the scolder has blown off the surplus feeling which vents itself in this way. There are times, indeed, when words may be multiplied to advantage in explaining to a child the nature and consequences of his offense, and the reasons why he should do differently in the future; but such words should always be spoken in gentleness, and in self-controlled earnestness. Scolding—rapidly spoken censure and protest, in the exhibit of strong feeling—is never in order as a means of training and directing a child."

6. Being Inconsistent with Discipline

"Therefore, I was not vacillating when I intended to do this, was I? Or that which I purpose, do I purpose according to the flesh, that with me there should be yes, yes and no, no at the same time? But as God is faithful, our word to you is not yes and no" (2 Cor. 1:17, 18).

"Because the sentence against an evil deed is not executed quickly, therefore the hearts of the sons of men among them are given fully to do evil" (Eccl. 8:11).

Parents commonly discipline inconsistently in two ways. The

first is by having different parental standards of discipline. For example, Father spanks and Mother talks. Father believes that a certain behavior is wrong. Mother sees nothing wrong with that same behavior. As a rule, it is better for one parent to tighten up a bit and the other to loosen up a little to unify their approach to discipline. Otherwise, children may become confused by their parents' different philosophies or methodologies of child rearing. The time, effort, and thought it will take for parents biblically to fine tune their parenting to the same specifics will be a valuable (and necessary) investment that should save hours of frustrating and ineffective discipline in years to come.

The second way that parents discipline inconsistently is by vacillating from day to day on either what is or what is not punishable behavior, and/or on how severe the chastisement will be. Children ought to know that their parents "yes" means "yes" and their "no" means "no." They should know that each offense will be treated justly and equitably regardless of their parents' emotional, spiritual, or physical condition at the time of discipline [7].

7. Having Double Standards

"The things you have learned and received and heard and seen in me, practice these things; and the God of peace shall be with you" (Phil. 4:9).

A parent who uses the Bible to teach, reprove, correct, and instruct his children in righteousness, but is not willing to practice that same biblical righteousness in his own life, is not only a hypocrite but a provoker of his children. "Do as I say, not as I do" is communicated more often by actions (or lack of them) than by words. Regardless of how this message is communicated, when children see their parents (their spiritual leaders) using double standards, that encourages their anger, much like the hypocrisy of the scribes and the Pharisees (the spiritual leaders of His day) rightly angered Christ.

8. Being Legalistic

The legalism I am referring to is that strain which elevates man-made rules to the same level of culpability as those commands which God has given in Scripture. God has given each set of Christian parents the responsibility to develop from Scripture a biblically based economy or "law of the house" for their children to abide by. This collection of house rules contains two basic sections:

The Law of The House

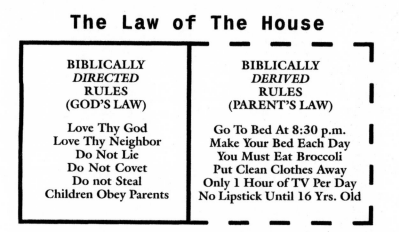

BIBLICALLY *DIRECTED* RULES (GOD'S LAW)	BIBLICALLY *DERIVED* RULES (PARENT'S LAW)
Love Thy God	Go To Bed At 8:30 p.m.
Love Thy Neighbor	Make Your Bed Each Day
Do Not Lie	You Must Eat Broccoli
Do Not Covet	Put Clean Clothes Away
Do not Steal	Only 1 Hour of TV Per Day
Children Obey Parents	No Lipstick Until 16 Yrs. Old

Figure 4. The Law of the House

Biblically directed rules are those which all men are obligated to obey because God commands them in His Word. Some obvious examples would be: Love Your God, Love Your Neighbor as Yourself, Do not lie, Do not covet, Do not steal, etc. On the other hand, *biblically derived rules* are those which are based on biblical principles; but which I am obligated to obey only as long as I am under God-ordained authority, in this case the authority of parents over their children. Examples might be: Do not stay up past 8:30 p.m. on school nights, Do not leave the table without asking to be excused, Eat all of your broccoli, You can only watch one hour of television per day and that only after your homework is finished.

Parents *must* develop temporal rules particular to their household in order to promote unity in a household of sinners. This necessity, however, can turn into neglect if the distinction between these man made temporary rules and God's eternal ones are not clearly delineated. This negligence often produces children who misunderstand, and consequently reject true Christianity. They can grow up with an overall impression which leads them to conclude that "Christianity" is an antiquated, stale, rigid, and nitpicking religion, having never experienced it's power to transform lives.

Christ often contended with this same kind of legalism with the religious leaders of His day. The scribes and the Pharisees held to, propogated, and esteemed the oral tradition, the Talmud, to such an extent that it became for them as legal and binding as the Scriptures. It may not have been wrong for them to follow their own man-made applications of Scripture ("He who observes the day, observes it for the Lord, and he who eats, does so for the Lord, for he gives thanks to God; and he who eats not, for the Lord he does not eat, and gives thanks to God." Rom. 14:6), but as soon as they imposed their man-made traditions on others, teaching these rules as though they were as obligatory as God's Law, they became bound up in legalism. It was to these leaders, who did not distinguish man-made rules from God-breathed commandments, that Christ, after calling them hypocrites, reiterated the words of Isaiah:

"This people honors me with their lips, but their heart is far from me. But in vain do they worship Me, teaching as doctrines the precepts of men" (Matt. 15:8-9).

If this kind of legalism provoked righteous indignation in the Lord Jesus, this kind of legalism can provoke anger in your child.

There is an important distinction that parents must make between these two sections of "The Law of the House." Whereas God's Law may never be appealed, parental laws are appealable. You may not say dogmatically (without being legalistic), "It's God's will for all children not to wear lipstick until they are sixteen years old." You may however say (if you're so inclined), "These are our house rules. If you would like to make a respectful appeal based on extenuating circumstances, we will consider it. When you are an adult, you will have your own house rules for your children. In the meantime, it is your responsibility to obey the house rules we have established based on biblical principles. If you decide to let your children wear lipstick at an earlier age, we will not interfere or tell you your decision is wrong." You cannot make a promise like that to your child when he or she violates a clear command of Scripture. To do so would mean you are promising not to obey the clear command in Matthew 18:15 yourself.

9. Not Admitting You're Wrong and Not Asking For Forgiveness

"If therefore you are presenting your offering at the altar, and there remember your brother has something against you, leave your offering there before the altar, and go your way; first be reconciled to your brother, and then come and present your offering" (Matt. 5:23, 24).

"Therefore confess your sins to one another and pray for one another..." (James 5:16).

A parent's failure to acknowledge offenses committed against his children (and others whom they know you've offended) often discourages the children from practicing open biblical communication. When children perceive such insensitivity and pride in their parents, they may wrongly conclude, "It's no use trying to talk to him, he'll never admit to doing anything wrong." Of course, the criteria for such communication should not be whether or not Dad will hear him, but rather, whether or not the offense is of such a nature that it cannot be overlooked (Prov. 19:11) or covered in love (Prov. 10:12; 17:9). In other words, your children should be taught to follow Matthew 18:15-17 as a necessary aspect in the relationship with you their parents, regardless of your parental response. In order to avoid provoking your children to anger in matters of offenses, I urge you to observe figure 5. for a four-step biblical approach to seeking forgiveness when you offend your child (or anyone else for that matter), and to read Appendix A., "What Does It Mean to Forgive?", page 179, for more on this subject vital to proper biblical parenting.

How to Ask For Forgiveness

1. *Acknowledge that you have sinned:*

"I was wrong," or "God has convinced me that I was wrong..."

2. *Identify the specific sin by its biblical name:*

"What I did was selfish," or "What I did was dishonest."

3. *Identify a biblical behavior to demonstrate your resolve to repent:*

"I should have clarified what you meant before I jumped to that hasty conclusion."
"The next time I will tell the truth no matter how afraid I might be of the consequences."

4. *Ask for forgiveness:*

"Will you forgive me?"

Figure 5. The Biblical Model for Asking for Forgiveness

10. Constantly Finding Fault

"Elihu's anger ... burned against Job ... And his anger burned against his three friends, because they had found no answer, and yet had condemned Job" (Job 32:2, 3).

Elihu became righteously indignant as he observed Job's three friends condemn him without accurately pinpointing exactly what he had done wrong. What I am addressing here is not the parental responsibility to point out sinful behavior and character deficiencies in the child, but rather the critical, condemning, accusing, judgmental attitude that so often accompanies legitimate attempts at reproof. I am referring to the kind of "spirit" that leads a child to believe that his parents are never or rarely pleased with him.

When the Lord Jesus was reproving the Ephesian church for losing her first love, He began with a list of those behaviors that pleased Him (Rev. 2). Perhaps the most effective safeguard against this provocation is for parents to purpose to praise, commend, and acknowledge biblical achievement with greater frequency than they reprove. This is not to imply a reduction in the number of reproofs, but rather to suggest an increase in the number of commendations. If you are a parent who has a tendency to nitpick about everything, I suggest that you memorize and meditate upon the following:

"A man's discretion makes him slow to anger, and it is his glory to overlook a transgression" (Proverbs 19:11).

Remember that although you have the responsibility to identify character flaws in your children for the purpose of training and correction, it is not always necessary to turn every non-characterological (habitual) sin into a mini-sermon.

11. Parents Reversing God-Given Roles

"Wives, be subject to your own husbands, as to the Lord. For the husband is the head of the wife, as Christ also is the head of the church, He Himself being the Savior of the body. But as the church is subject to Christ, so also the wives ought to be to their husbands in everything" (Ephesians 5:22-24).

When God's order in the home is violated, various consequences tend to be set in motion. These consequences create a home environment that promotes frustration. Wives tend to become embittered over husbands not managing their homes as the Bible directs. Husbands tend to become embittered and lose respect for wives who are not fulfilling their God given roles.

Both husband and wife may struggle with the guilt that so often occurs whenever biblical roles are reversed. Children who know what the Bible teaches about such things tend to view their parents' relationship as a double standard. They may even resent their mother for usurping her husband's authority, or their father for not managing his home well— or both. In addition, children may be uncertain and confused about their own gender roles. They may not want to model their parents behavior but have no other first-hand examples to follow. All of these consequences can frustrate children and provoke them to anger.

12. Not Listening to Your Child's Opinion or Taking His or Her "Side of the Story" Seriously

"He who gives an answer before he hears, it is folly and shame to him" (Prov. 18:3).

"The first to plead his case seems just, until another comes and examines him" (Prov. 18:17).

You may not always agree with your child's reasoning, conclusions and opinions, but if you are going to lead him into the truth, you will need to understand his perspective. Moreover, by not attempting to understand his perspective, you may communicate such sinful attitudes as arrogance, impatience, apathy, or lack of love. People of all ages are inclined to translate rejection of their ideas as rejection of their persons. Naturally, children should be taught how to receive reproof biblically and learn not to equate rejection of one's ideas as personal rejection. When, however, there is a constant barrage of parental insensitivity in this area, children quickly conclude that Mom and Dad, like the proverbial fool, are not interested in anything but their own opinions.

13. Comparing Them to Others

" For we are not bold to class or compare ourselves with some of those who commend themselves; but when they measure themselves

41

by themselves, and compare themselves with themselves, they are without understanding" (2 Cor. 10:12).

God gives every child unique gifts and talents. Adam gave every child (through the transmission of sin Rom. 5:16-19) a heart that is disposed to all manner of evil thoughts and intents. A child should learn at an early age "not to think more highly of himself than he ought to think; but to think so as to have sound judgment, as God has allotted to each a measure of faith" (Rom. 12:3).

Parents, on the other hand should take Paul's warning in 2 Corinthians 10:12 to heart and avoid comparing their children (favorably or unfavorably) to other children. Proper biblical comparisons may be made in the following two directions:

Forward looking— by comparing where the child is today to the biblical standard of maturity as demonstrated in Jesus Christ (Eph. 4:13-15; 2 Cor. 3:18), or—

Backward looking— by comparing the child's spiritual maturity today to his own spiritual maturity at various points in the past (2 Peter 1:3-12; Rev. 2:2-5).

14. Not Making Time "Just to Talk"

"Be quick to listen, slow to speak" (James 1:19).
"There is a time to keep silent, and a time to speak" (Eccl. 3:7).

Relationships are impossible to build without communication. To the degree (and only to the degree) that God has revealed Himself to us in the Bible, can we have a relationship with Him. As parents and children alike reveal themselves to each other through various communication forms, their relationships with each other are strengthened. Revelation of oneself is a biblical prerequisite for effective relationships.

When Mom and Dad allow the pressures and pleasures of life to keep them from spending enough time in the revelation/communication process, strong parent/child relationships are not established. In addition to provoking children to wrath, this weakening of the parent/child relationship motivates children to build closer relationships with friends instead of parents.

15. Not Praising or Encouraging Your Child

"I know your deeds and your toil and perseverance, and that you cannot endure evil men, and you put to the test those who call themselves apostles, and they are not, and you found them (to be) false; and you have perseverance and have endured for My name's sake, and have not grown weary. But I have (this) against you, that you have left your first love" (Rev 2:2-4).

It is significant that the Lord Jesus Christ, when He reproved the church at Ephesus, began with praise. When a Christian evaluates himself (as every person does continually), it is important for him to evaluate himself accurately. An accurate self-perception involves a clear understanding not only of what is wrong and needs to be corrected, but also of what is right and pleasing to God. Too often parents focus only on the wrong, and consequently, their children tend to evaluate themselves inaccurately. Their self-perceptions become distorted rather than sober (Rom. 12:3) and true (Phil. 4:8). I suggest to parents that they learn to keep their children regularly bathed in a solution of praise so that when reproof and correction are administered, these measures will be perceived as one more element of balanced biblical love.

16. Failing to Keep Your Promises

"But let your statement be, 'Yes, yes' or 'No, no'; and anything beyond these is of evil" (Matt. 5:37).

"He swears to his own hurt and does not change (his promise)... He who does these things will never be shaken" (Ps. 15:4-5).

"Do not lie to one another, since you laid aside the old self with its evil practices" (Col. 3:9).

Promises and commitments are usually made with every intention of keeping them and no intent to deceive. However, when promises and commitments consistently are not kept, regardless of the reason, and an attempt is not made to break the contract biblically (see Prov. 6:1-5) or forgiveness is not sought from a child for breach of contract, his disappointment turns into anger. As the string of broken promises gets longer and longer, and the child increasingly views his parents as undependable, unreliable, and deceitful, his anger may intensify proportionately.

Many responses may occur in the heart of a child whose hopes have been dashed by broken promises. Unless children are taught appropriate biblical responses, they may struggle with some of the following emotions:

▶ *Disappointment and discouragement*
▶ *Suspicion and cynicism— unwillingness to trust*
▶ *Rejection— hurt feelings*
▶ *Bitterness and resentment*
▶ *Loss of respect or contempt for parents*
▶ *Thoughts of being unloved*

Any of these, if not dealt with biblically, can easily lead to anger and then to rebellion.

17. Chastening in Front of Others

"And if your brother sins, go and reprove him in private; if he listens to you, you have won your brother" (Matt. 18:15).

Why do so many Christian parents overlook one of the most foundational discipline passages in the Bible? Perhaps it is because when we read the word "brother," we immediately think of some church member with whom we have had or are currently involved in a conflict. Regardless of the reason, our Lord's instruction in Matthew 18:15-20, when properly applied to the family conflict, will safeguard each member from abuse and will prevent sinful actions from becoming sinful habits. Remember, your believing son or daughter is primarily and permanently your brother. He is secondarily, and temporarily your child.

The disciplinary principle derived from this verse is that the circle of confession and correction should only be as large as the circle of offense. If your child sins in the presence of others, he may in certain cases be verbally rebuked (but not physically chastised) in their presence. If the sin however is not public, the disciplinary process should be handled between the parent and child. To violate the clear instruction of Christ by disciplining a child in front of others for sins he has committed in private is to sin against God and the child.

18. Not Allowing Enough Freedom

"The wisdom from above is first pure, then peaceable, gentle, reasonable (easy to be entreated), full of mercy..." (James 3:17).

"And from everyone who has been given much shall much be required; and to whom is entrusted much, of him they will ask all the more" (Luke 12:48).

Children, rather than expecting their parents to simply hand them freedom on a silver platter, ought to be willing to earn freedom by demonstrating that they are faithful. Faithfulness involves demonstrating to God and others that you can be trusted with increasing freedom based on at least two things: the successful fulfillment of specific responsibilities and the successive competence to make biblically wise decisions.

When children start demonstrating such faithfulness and parents do not reward them with the freedom and the trust commensurate with their achievement, they can become exasperated, discouraged, and even give up. Common reasons why parents do not give their children enough freedom include: overprotectiveness, insecurity, fear, unbiblical standards based on tradition rather than Scripture, inordinate desires to have perfect children, and inordinate concern for what others might think. By not rewarding faithfulness with requisite freedom, parents may hinder a form of motivation that is inherently biblical— the desire to earn trust.

19. Allowing Too Much Freedom

"The rod and reproof give wisdom but a child who gets his own way brings shame to his mother" (Prov. 29:15).

"...But he (the child) is under guardians and managers until the date set by the father" (Gal. 4:1,2).

When children are allowed to (1) habitually practice any sinful behavior, or (2) participate in non-sinful activities before demonstrating the appropriate levels of responsibility and maturity (i.e. having the freedom to dispose of great sums of money without knowing how to live by a biblically balanced budget), or (3) live an undisciplined life, being allowed to do almost anything their heart desires with instant gratification, other problems develop. Children must be taught how to repent of sin, how to be responsible, and how to live a self-disciplined life. Parents will suffer along with their children if they neglect these disciplinary responsibilities.

Children can soon come to know the truth that God equates discipline with love:

"For those whom the Lord loves He disciplines, and He scourges every son whom he receives. It is for discipline that you endure: God deals with you as with sons; for what son is there whom his father does not discipline? But if you are without discipline, of which all have become partakers, then you are illegitimate children and not sons. Furthermore we had earthly fathers to discipline us and we respected them; shall we not much rather be subject to the Father of spirits and live?" (Heb. 12:6-9).

Children who grow up in homes with too much freedom and not enough discipline may quickly conclude that they are not truly loved by their parents.

20. Mocking Your Child

"My spirit is broken, my days are extinguished, the grave is ready for me. Surely mockers are with me, and my eye gazes on their provocation" (Job 17:1-2).

Provocative Parents

"And the LORD said to him, 'Who has made man's mouth? Or who makes him dumb or deaf, or seeing or blind? Is it not I, the LORD?'" (Exodus 4:11).

Parents should never ridicule or mock. I am especially concerned about two categories of teasing. First, you should not make fun of inadequacies about which the child can do nothing. Parents should never ridicule a child for things that have nothing to do with pleasing God. Examples from this category include a child's intelligence, athletic abilities, physical features, and motor coordination. These are personal characteristics that are not sinful. According to Exodus 4:11 and Psalm 139:13-16, God takes responsibility for prescribing these traits in each person before birth.

The second thing you should not do is make fun of things that are sinful. Should Christians make fun of things that God sent His Son to die for? Sin isn't a laughing matter. Sinful behavior in children, especially those that are habitual, should be addressed with sobriety not with frivolity.

21. Abusing Them Physically

"A bishop (overseer), then must be. . . not violent. . . , but gentle" (1 Tim. 3:3 NKJV, my translation in parenthesis).

"When the donkey saw the angel of the LORD, she lay down under Balaam; so Balaam was angry and struck the donkey with his stick. And the LORD opened the mouth of the donkey, and she said to Balaam, 'What have I done to you, that you have struck me these three times?' Then Balaam said to the donkey, 'Because you have made a mockery of me! If there had been a sword in my hand, I would have killed you by now'" (Num. 22:27-29).

When Balaam became angry at his donkey for not meeting his expectations, he struck the beast with a stick. Balaam went on to say that if he had a sword he would have killed the donkey. Children, of course, are not beasts. Angry parents, however, may be guilty of treating them as such when their anger is out of control. Several parallels can be made between Balaam's sinful anger and a parent out of control. I will mention three:

1. Balaam struck the donkey in haste, before he had collected all of the relevant data. Before we as parents jump to hasty and unfounded conclusions and discipline our children for the wrong reason, we must be certain we have all the facts.

2. Balaam struck the donkey because the donkey embarrassed him. We should be certain that our motivation for discipline is biblical, and not selfish. For us to discipline our children for selfish reasons, such as embarrassment or unfulfilled expectations, rather than for sin, is vindictive and abusive.

3. Balaam was out of control. (He would have killed his faithful donkey if he had the means to do it!) We parents should discipline our children only when we have gotten our anger under control and are not likely to harm our children.

22. Ridiculing or Name Calling

"Let no unwholesome word proceed out of your mouth, but only such a word as is good for edification according to the need of the moment, that it may give grace to those who hear" (Eph. 4:29).

You may think: "Now wait a minute. Jesus called people names, so did Paul, as well as many of the biblical authors. Why can't I call my children names?" Well, I suppose you can, provided your name calling meets biblical criteria. The only names you ought to be using to describe your children (or any other person for that matter) are names that the Bible uses to describe categories of people. Even legitimate biblical name-calling should only be used when there is enough evidence to suggest the category.

Categories such as slothful, foolish, double-minded, deceitful, self-centered, and idolatrous are names that God uses to identify those individuals who have so given themselves over to a particular sin that their life is dominated and characterized by that sin. Names like Idiot, Moron, Dummy, Meathead, Dingbat, Fatty, Shorty, and Pinhead don't fit biblical criteria.

Additionally, using biblical names to describe sinful behavior should be employed only when a child's life displays a particular sin to such a degree that the sin is obviously affecting various areas of his life (home, school, church, social, health, etc.) When it is necessary to show a child that his life is taking on unacceptable characteristics, the biblical name should be used as a didactic tool, not as a weapon. As a tool the name serves to motivate the child to change. As a weapon, the name embarrasses, shames, or antagonizes the child and is primarily punitive in nature. Punitive name calling provokes anger in children.

23. Unrealistic Expectations

"When I was a child I used to speak as a child, think as a child, reason as a child" (1 Cor. 13:11).

The Bible acknowledges that children think, speak and reason differently from adults. The process whereby children grow and develop takes time. Additionally, children grow at different rates. These factors need to be considered by parents as they establish expectations for their children.

Parents should not impose standards or expectations upon their children that their children are developmentally incapable of performing. Appropriate standards and expectations are clearly delineated in Scripture. Our emphasis should be on character not achievement. For example, godly character is shown in doing your best for God's glory, not by getting straight A's in school. Factored into the equation should also be the reality that children are sinners and are therefore going to sin. Hence, it should not be surprising to parents when even children with agreeable dispositions occasionally show their sinful hearts.

24. Practicing Favoritism

"Now his older son was in the field, and when he came and approached the house, he heard music and dancing. And he summoned one of the servants and (began) inquiring what these things might be.

And he said to him, 'Your brother has come, and your father has killed the fattened calf, because he has received him back safe and sound.' <u>But he became angry</u>, and was not willing to go in; and his father came out and (began) entreating him. But he answered and said to his father, 'Look! For so many years I have been serving you, and I have never neglected a command of yours; and (yet) you have never given me a kid, that I might be merry with my friends; but when this son of yours came, who has devoured your wealth with harlots, you killed the fattened calf for him'" (Luke 15:25-30; emphasis added).

When the prodigal's elder brother perceived (wrongly) that his father was showing favoritism toward his younger brother, he became angry. Since siblings are different, they should be treated as individuals. The standard, however, by which each child is evaluated and by which parents respond to each child *should be identical*, a point the elder brother did not understand and so he misinterpreted his father's motive.

Consider a thermometer as an illustration.— When placed in a refrigerator, it may read 38 degrees F°, when placed on the kitchen table— 72 degrees, when placed in an oven however, it may read 400 degrees! Did the thermometer ever change? Did it ever stop faithfully measuring temperature? Did it ever stop being a thermometer and become a wrist watch? Of course not! What changed is not the thermometer, but rather its environment or circumstances. Likewise, when a child observes a certain parental treatment a sibling is receiving while in a different set of circumstances than himself, he needs to be assured that he or she will be treated in a similar manner (with justice) by his parent(s) should he find himself in the same or a similar set of circumstances.

25. Child Training with Worldy Methodologies Inconsistent with God's Word

"And, fathers, do not provoke your children to anger; <u>but bring them up in the discipline and instruction of the Lord</u>" (Eph. 6:4; emphasis added).

Did you notice the word "but" in Ephesians 6:4? Two ways are being contrasted. Raising your child properly in the discipline and instruction of the Lord will not provoke him to anger, but employing the counsel and instruction of man-made pop psychology almost certainly will. The use of behavior modification and cognitive therapy techniques that were designed to replace Christ and the Scriptures with human wisdom (Prov. 16:25) cannot produce in an angry child the fruit of the Spirit. That is what is necessary to displace his characterological anger. Make certain that all means and methods of child training you use can be Scripturally validated. Only then will you avoid provoking your child to anger and truly bring him up in the discipline and instruction of the Lord.

Well, how did you do? How many ways have you and your spouse been provoking your children to anger? Remember, the anger is your child's sin, but you are 100% responsible before God for the sins which provoked him to that anger. If you recognize that you have exasperated and provoked your children, I urge you to immediately take the following steps (see figure 6. below) to begin creating a home environment that will help them to replace anger with the love, kindness, gentleness, and forgiveness of Christ.

Repenting from Provoking Children To Anger

1. *Identify* the specific ways you have been provoking your child to anger: Read Eph. 6:4.

2. *Confess* these sins to God: Read 1 John 1:9.

3. *Ask* your child's forgiveness for your sins against him: Read Acts 24:16; Review point #9 of this chapter.

4. *Develop* a plan with your child's assistance to replace those sinful behaviors with their biblical alternatives: Read Proverbs 28:13.

5. *Consider* specific ways you can provoke your children to love and good works: Read Hebrews 10:24.

Figure 6. Repenting from Provoking Children to Anger

Angry Attitudes

By the time I was ready to see Joshua for the first time (after having two or three previous sessions with his parents) I was able to persuade him without much difficulty that he was angry. I have found that most angry individuals readily acknowledge their anger problem. According to Proverbs 14:10, "The heart knows its own bitterness."

I began our session by explaining to Jim, Linda and Joshua the two extremes of sinful anger— ventilation and internalization. Walking over to the white board, I explained the two extremes with the help of Jay Adams' popular illustration.

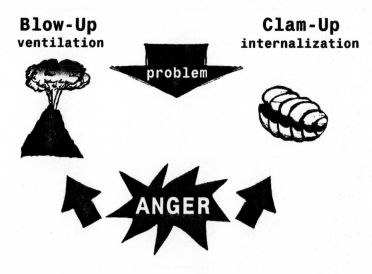

Figure 7. The Two Sinful Extremes of Anger

Angry Attitudes

I then explained, "When faced with a problem there is the possibility for everyone to become angry. Anger has potential to be good or bad (righteous or sinful.) There are two extreme manifestations of sinful anger to which people often resort. On one end of the spectrum is *internalization*. Some people 'clam up' when they get angry. These individuals withdraw emotionally, cry, pout, sulk, retreat to another room, go for a drive (without first committing to resolve the conflict later), and employ a "cold shoulder" tactic.

"At the other end of the spectrum is *ventilation.* The fool gives full vent to his anger (Prov. 29:11). Some people 'blow up' when they get angry. These individuals resort to raising their voice, name calling, using profanity, throwing, hitting and kicking things, the use of biting sarcasm, and various other acts of vengeance. Some people blow-up first then clam-up, others clam-up until the internal pressure builds to overflowing at which time they blow-up."

At this point I asked each member of the family to examine and acknowledge his tendencies to blow-up or clam-up. Then I asked them to identify the specific ways those tendencies are manifested. As each family member identified specific ways of responding, I tried to help them see the consequences of their responses.

"Anger is an emotion God gives to us for the purpose of destroying something. If we clam-up," I asked Linda, who was prone to internalize, "who are we destroying with our anger?"

"Ourselves!"

"And if we blow up," I asked Jim, who had a penchant towards ventilation, "who are we destroying with our anger?"

"The person at whom we blow up!"

"Exactly right!" [8]

Referring them back to Adams' diagram, I asked, "What do you suppose God wants you to destroy with this anger?"

"The *problem*!," Joshua responded.

"That's right! God expects us to release our anger under His control toward the problem."

Completing the diagram, I explained further. (See Figure 8.)

"Have you ever noticed that usually when we get angry it involves another person? Since most of our problems involve other people, one thing is almost always necessary to transfer the anger from our hearts to the problem. Do you know what that is?"

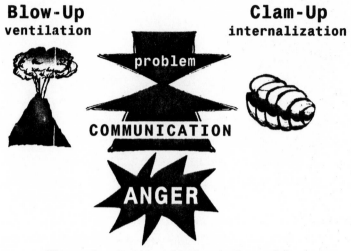

Figure 8.   Communication is Essential

"I guess we have to talk about it," Joshua replied.

"That's right! Communication is necessary in order to get the problem solved. That means that if you as a family are going to solve your anger problems, you must learn how to communicate. In fact, I don't believe you will ever solve your anger problems, without making it your goal to become proficient in biblical communication skills."

If Christians should be proficient at any thing, they should be proficient at communication. You may find it surprising that you, as a Christian, are commanded to communicate in at least 45 different ways in the New Testament epistles. These ways to communicate are from the New Testament epistles alone, not including the rest of the New Testament and Old Testament, and do not include examples or principles of communication found throughout the Bible. Volumes could be and should be written on this subject. However, for the purpose of this book, only a few appropriate concepts will be addressed, some in this chapter, others in chapters to follow.

The Communication Pie

I continued my presentation with what I call the communication pie diagram.

"As I am standing here talking to you, I am communicating to you with much more than just my words. I am also communicating with the tone of my voice and with my non-verbal communication. All three of these elements play a vital part in face-to-face communication."

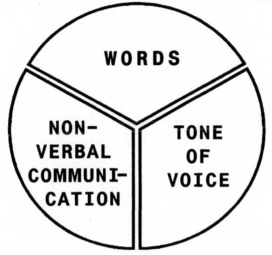

Figure 9. "The Communication Pie"

Because the Bible addresses all aspects of communication, the Christian should make it his goal to become proficient in all three areas. First, we must consider the words themselves. Our words should be given the most emphasis since the Bible speaks so frequently about their importance. 'The words of the wise are as goads' (Eccl. 12:11, see also 1 Cor. 2:13, Eph. 4:29). The following are examples of the power of words:

With words... people can be motivated, encouraged, pierced, or healed.
With words... conflicts can be resolved and people's problems can be solved.

The Heart of Anger

With words... precise meaning is communicated.
With words... God reveals himself to man.
With words... we communicate the Gospel to others.
With words... our minds comprehend the truth of God.
With the words of Scripture... which have been internalized by the Christian, the Holy Spirit works to transform our lives into the image of Christ.
With words... the man of God brings doctrine, reproof, correction, and instruction in righteousness.
With words... man will be justified.
With words... man will be condemned.

If there is ever a time when a believer ought to premeditate what he is going to say, it is in those circumstances when he is most likely to become angry. When a man is angry (or experiencing other intense emotions), he is at greatest risk of sinning with his words. Children must be taught to choose their words carefully, especially when a problem exists that makes them angry:

"The heart of the righteous studies how to answer" (Prov. 15:28).

"The heart of the wise teaches his mouth and adds learning to his lips" (Prov. 16:23).

The second slice of the communication pie is tone of voice. The Bible addresses this form of communication also:

"A soft answer turns away wrath" (Prov. 15:1).

"Sweetness of the lips increases persuasiveness" (Prov. 16:21).

It is not enough for us to choose the right words. We must say the right words in a tone that is appropriate.

Children probably provoke their parents to anger more quickly by being disrespectful than by any other behavior. Yet, it is more often the tone of voice of the child rather than the words that communicates disrespect. Disrespect, of course, is not the only attitude communicated by tone of voice. For instance, rage, bitterness, vengeance, shame, fear and other attitudes that are often present along side of anger are often communicated by inflection.

Angry Attitudes

The point I am about to make is more easily done in person than in print, but I will attempt, with the help of a thesaurus, to make it here as best I can. At this juncture in my counseling interview I prompted Joshua to ask me a question that could be answered with a yes or no answer.

"Do you like being a counselor?" Joshua asked.

"Yes," I responded with a pleasant, warm, friendly, cheerful, lighthearted and pleasing tone of voice— as if to say, "I enjoy counseling so much that it is one of my greatest delights because I get to see people grow and change and solve their problems!"

"Now," I continued, "Ask me the same question once again."

"Do you like being a counselor?"

"YES!" I responded, this time with a tone of voice that was loud, abrupt, harsh, gruff, rude, caustic, angry, scathing and cutting— as if to say, "That is the dumbest question I have ever heard! Do you really think I would put up with little brats like you if I didn't like my job?!"

I hope you get the picture. My clients usually do. The effect of tone of voice is so great that some experts believe it to be up to seven times more powerful in certain situations than the words themselves.

"The third slice of the communication pie is non-verbal communication. Non-verbal communication includes facial expressions (countenance), gestures, eye contact, posture, spatial relationship and touch (when appropriate)."

Once again the Bible has much to say about communicating non-verbally. The scope of our discussion, however, does not allow for the development of each element. I would like to comment on facial expressions, however, because of their biblical significance.

Did you know that feelings of pride, anger, bitterness, fear, sensuality, and rebellion can all show on our faces, without our even being aware of it? The following are eight attitudes which mar a person's countenance along with the biblical references which explain how these attitudes are related to one's facial expressions:

Eight Attitudes of the Heart That Can Mar the Countenance

1. Pride The wicked, in the haughtiness of his countenance, does not seek (Him). All his thoughts are, "There is no God" (Psalm 10:4).

2. Anger But for Cain and for his offering He had no regard. So Cain became very angry and his countenance fell (Gen. 4:5).

3. Bitterness Now Jacob heard the words of Laban's sons... And Jacob saw the attitude (face or countenance) of Laban, and behold, it was not (friendly) toward him as formerly (Gen. 31:1-2).

4. Fear Suddenly the fingers of a man's hand emerged and began writing opposite the lampstand on the plaster of the wall of the king's palace, and the king saw the back of the hand that did the writing. Then the king's face grew pale, and his thoughts alarmed him; and his hip joints went slack, and his knees began knocking together (Dan. 5:5).

5. Sensuality Do not desire her beauty in your heart, Nor let her catch you with her eyelids (Prov. 6:25).

6. Rebellion The eye that mocks a father, and scorns a mother, the ravens of the valley will pick it out, and the young eagles will eat it (Prov. 30:17).

7. Guilt And I said, "O my God, I am ashamed and embarrassed to lift up my face to Thee, my God, for our iniquities have risen above our heads, and our guilt has grown even to the heavens. Since the days of our fathers to this day we (have been) in great guilt, and on account of our iniquities we, our kings (and) our priests have been given into the hand of the kings of the lands, to the sword, to captivity, and to plunder and to open shame, as (it is) this day" (Ezra 9:6-7).

8. Selfishness Do not eat the bread of a selfish man (literally: a man who has an evil eye) (Prov. 23:6).

Figure 10. Attitudes Which Mar The Countenance

Angry Attitudes

The opposite holds true also though:

"A man's wisdom makes his face to shine and the harshness of his countenance to be changed." (Eccl. 8:1)

Changing facial expressions is probably the most difficult aspect of communication to correct. This is true largely because we are often unaware of what our countenance is doing at any moment. One can comprehend the meaning of his own words as he articulates them and he can hear the tone of his voice as he expresses meaning, but he cannot see the look on his face, unless he stands in front of a mirror or records his communication on video tape (a good idea for helping children improve communication skills). Therefore we must rely on feedback from others to help us fine tune our non-verbal communication. Consequently, children need their parents' feedback in learning how to express their thoughts in times of anger.

Before continuing with additional ways to help angry children overcome their anger, it will be necessary to explain the meaning of a word which everybody knows but which few understand. The word is discipline. It is a word that expresses an essential prerequisite for biblical change to take place.

Discipline:
What It Really Means

> *Question:* What is the first rule for teaching a parakeet how to talk?
> *Answer:* You must have a larger vocabulary than the parakeet.
>
> ---
>
> *Question:* What is the first rule for disciplining children?
> *Answer:* You must have more discipline than the child.

Many of the parents with whom I work have forgotten (or never realized in the first place) that their ability to train (discipline) their children effectively is directly related to the self-discipline they possess as trainers. The more disciplined a parent is, the more likely he will be able to succeed at child training. In this chapter, I will explain what it means to be disciplined. As you read this chapter, consider the degree to which you are self-disciplined; it is only to *that degree* that you can expect to succeed in disciplining your child to correct his anger problem.

H. Clay Trumbull makes a distinction between two often confused concepts:

"The term 'training,' like the term 'teaching', is used in various senses; hence it is liable to be differently understood by different persons, when applied to a single department of a parent's duties in the bringing up of his children. Indeed, the terms 'training' and 'teaching' are often used interchangeably, as covering the entire process of a child's education. In this sense, a child's training is understood to include his teaching; and, again, his teaching is understood to include his training. But in its more restricted sense, the training of a child is the shaping, the developing, and the controlling of his personal faculties and powers; while the teaching of a child is the securing to him of knowledge from beyond himself.

It has been said that the essence of teaching is causing another to know. It may similarly be said that the essence of training is causing another to do. Teaching gives knowledge. Training gives skill. Teaching fills the mind. Training shapes the habits. Teaching brings to the child that which he did not have before. Training enables a child to make use of that which is already his possession. We teach a child the meaning of words. We train a child in speaking and walking. We teach him the truths which we have learned for ourselves. We train him in habits of study, that he may be able to learn other truths for himself. Training and teaching must go on together in the wise upbringing of any and every child. The one will fail of its own best end if it be not accompanied by the other. He who knows how to teach a child, is not competent for the oversight of a child's education unless he also knows how to train a child.

Training is a possibility long before teaching is. Before a child is old enough to know what is said to it, it is capable of feeling, and of conforming to, or of resisting the pressure of efforts for its training. A child can be trained to go to sleep in the arms of its mother or nurse, or in a cradle, or on a bed; with rocking, or without it; in a light room, or in a dark one; in a noisy room, or only in a quiet one; to expect nourishment and to accept it only at fixed hours, or at its own fancy— while as yet it cannot understand any teaching concerning the importance or the fitness of one of these things. A very young child can be trained to cry for what it wants, or to keep quiet, as means of securing it. And, as a matter of fact, the training of children is begun much earlier than their teaching. Many a child is well started in its life-training by the time it is six weeks old; even though its elementary teaching is not attempted until months after that." [9]

The "Gumnazo" Principle

When I was growing up on Long Island, I was given, as one of my chores, the daily responsibility of sweeping the kitchen floor after supper. I was expected to do this task *whether I felt like it or not.* I did it repeatedly and regularly day in and day out for many years. I never really enjoyed sweeping, but went from hating it to tolerating it. As the years went by, I continued sweeping until I went to off to college. At last, I was finally liberated from "the bondage of the broom."

Twelve years ago, when I first came to Atlanta, I was preparing lunch in the basement kitchen of the church which had been graciously loaned to me for our first counseling office. Opening the pantry door, I discovered a pile of sugar in the middle of the closet floor. What do you suppose my next conscious thought was? If you are thinking "Sweep it up!" you are wrong. My next conscious thought came after I had walked out the kitchen door, walked down a long hallway, entered a utility closet, located a broom, left the closet, and was walking back down the hall again on my way to the kitchen with the broom in my hand. My next conscious thought was, "Lou, what are you doing? Nobody asked you to sweep the floor. No one is going to give you brownie points for sweeping the floor. You're sweeping the floor because it is the *right* thing to do."

The years I spent sweeping the kitchen floor as a youth, as well as the subsequent discipline I had gone through since then, had been used by God to develop a good habit. A habit is something that is practiced so frequently that it becomes "second nature." It is a routine that has become so natural that it can be accomplished quickly, easily, automatically, and (as in my case) unconsciously. I had, over the years, disciplined myself for the purpose of sweeping up a messy floor. Paul told Timothy to discipline himself for the purpose of godliness:

"But discipline yourself for the purpose of godliness" (1 Tim. 4:7).

The word *discipline* in the greek of the new testament scriptures is *gumnazo* (from which we get such words as gymnastics and gymnasium), it means to exercise or to train. The idea is that of a man who starts training with weights to increase his strength. The first day at the gym he attempts to lift 80 lbs., but finds he cannot get the barbell above his head. Consequently, he decides to start with only 50 lbs. He discovers that he can press the 50 lb. barbell 12 times over his head. He then continues to exercise with this weight for one week. The next week he increases the barbell weight to 60 lbs. He maintains the 60 lb. weight for seven days, then graduates to 70 lbs. All the while his muscles get stronger and larger. Week by week, he continues increasing the weight until after two years he is easily pressing over 175 lbs. On the two-year anniversary of his having begun weight-training, he walks over to the 80 lb. barbell, which he couldn't lift above his shoulders two years ago, and with one hand lifts it all the way over his head. His muscles have become so strong and so large that what was once impossible, has now become an easy feat,— because of training and exercise (*gumnazo*). This is exactly what happens when we exercise ourselves for the purpose of godliness. What once seemed impossible becomes easy (second nature).

Now what does all this have to do with children? Consider the following two verses from Hebrews and keep in mind the meaning of *gumnazo* as you read:

"For everyone who partakes only of milk is not accustomed to the word of righteousness, for he is a babe. But solid food is for the mature, who because of practice have their senses trained (gumnazo-ed) to discern good and evil" (Hebrews 5:13-14).

The context of these two verses is a rebuke. Some of the Hebrew Christians had not developed to the point of being teachers as they should have (with respect to the time they had been given to grow to maturity in Christ), and were now being rebuked. The biblical author uses developmental language to contrast the growth and training of children to the growth and training of Christians. He assumes that the reader understands an essential universal principle of child development that our culture seems to have forgotten—*training*. Two words in particular are employed to communicate this principle. I like to refer to it as The Gumnazo Principle. The word *gumnazo* is used again in this verse as it was used in 1 Timothy 4:7. Again its meaning "to train by exercise" can be clearly seen in this passage. The second word, which actually appears first in this text, is the word *exis*, which means "a habit or a practice that has been produced by continuous past exercise" so that it has become "second nature."

Next, let's consider Hebrews 12: 7-11:

"It is for discipline that you endure; God deals with you as with sons; for what son is there whom his father does not discipline? But if you are without discipline, of which all have become partakers, then you are illegitimate children and not sons. Furthermore, we had earthly fathers to discipline us, and we respected them; shall we not much rather be subject to the Father of spirits and live? For they disciplined us for a short time as seemed best to them, but He disciplines us for our good, that we may share His holiness. All discipline for the moment seems not to be joyful, but sorrowful; yet to those who have been trained (gumnazo-ed) by it, afterwards it yields the peaceful fruit of righteousness."

The context here is "how to handle a spanking from God." The author is exhorting his readers to endure chastening from the Lord, knowing that it will produce the "peaceable fruits of righteousness to those who have been exercised (*gumnazo-ed*) by it" (KJV). As we saw before, a contrast is made between how children respond to chastening by their fathers, and how Christians are to respond to chastening by their heavenly Father. Again, the author assumes some knowledge of that essential principle of child training I have referred to as The Gumnazo Principle.

Training Your Apprentice

The Gumnazo Principle can be illustrated by the example of a blacksmith who is training an apprentice. Apprenticeships are not as popular today as they were during the early days of our nation when Benjamin Franklin, for example, served as an apprentice for his older brother. Then, it was not uncommon for the apprentice to live with, be provided for, and be subject to the master craftsman. An apprenticeship was a thorough, intense training that usually lasted for seven years. Basically, it was training by practice, practice and more practice, until the apprentice got it right. The master craftsman would likely first explain and demonstrate the

Discipline: What It Really Means

equipment. Then he would allow the apprentice to observe him going through the entire process of making a horseshoe from lighting the forge to shoeing the horse's hoof with the finished product, explaining each procedure in great detail. After a number of observations, the master craftsman would allow the apprentice to help with some of the procedure. Instructing him, the master would allow the apprentice to try the procedure. He would correct him on the spot should he make a mistake, *and require him to do it again until he got it right.* The master may have stood behind his apprentice, holding or gripping his hands over the hands of the apprentice, as they would hold the iron in the fire until the iron had just the right glow of red. Then, *hand in hand*, the master craftsman and the apprentice would quickly bring the iron to the anvil; and *hand in hand*, the master would demonstrate to the apprentice just where to hammer the iron and just how hard to strike it. Then, he would put it back into the fire and so on until the horseshoe was complete. After a few exercises of this hands-on training, the master would be ready to allow the apprentice to try the procedure by himself. Still standing behind his student, he would observe the apprentice's work, noticing every detail of workmanship. Then, as soon as a mistake was made, *immediately* he might say, "No, this way." *Again grasping the hand* of the apprentice, he would show him precisely *how to correct his mistake.* That's The Gumnazo Principle in action!

Imagine what it would be like if the master craftsman had simply explained the procedure one time, and when the apprentice made his first mistake, the master said, "Wrong! No dinner for you tonight. You'd better improve tomorrow."

"That would be cruel, unmerciful, and a violation of education," you say.

Yet that is the way many Christian parents "discipline" their children. "That was disrespectful!" they say, as they cruelly slap the child across the face with the backside of a hand, while feeling good about the fact that they identified exactly what the child did wrong—being disrespectful.

The Gumnazo Principle maintains that you haven't disciplined a child properly until you have brought him to the point of repentance by requiring him to practice the biblical alternative to sinful behavior. This would involve not just asking forgiveness for the disrespect, not just identifying the sin by name (two essential steps in biblical discipline); but also by responding with a respectful alternative to the disrespect using the appropriate words, tone of voice, and non-verbal communication. The application of The Gumnazo Principle will be explained in more detail in the next chapter.

Imagine what it would be like trying to teach your son how to tie a double Windsor in his necktie or trying to teach your daughter how to make and roll out a pie crust without The Gumnazo Principle. At some point, unless you have unlimited time and resources, you would have to stop the process of verbal instruction and show your child how to correct a mistake. If the gumnazo principle is vital for teaching such relatively simple and temporal tasks, how much more is it necessary for teaching the application of eternal truth and the development of Christ-like character.

Before you begin the next chapter, be sure that you clearly understand The Gumnazo Principle; biblical discipline involves correcting wrong behavior by practicing right behavior, with the right attitude, for the right reason, until the right behavior becomes habitual.

Practicing Biblical Communication

Now we can combine the communication principles of Chapter Three with The Gumnazo Principle of Chapter Four. Suppose, after your child comes home from school one particular afternoon, you inquire how his day went. You walk over to the sofa where he is sitting. You notice that he is staring out the window.

"So, tell me— what's new and exciting or different at school today?" you ask.

Without lifting his gaze off of its locked position on the window, with his head turned away from you, his arms folded, his legs crossed in the opposite direction from where you are seated next to him, he blurts out in a curt, disgusted, sarcastic tone of voice,—

"Can't you see I'm thinking. Why don't you go away and bother somebody else!"

How would you respond?—

> *Get angry and say something equally sarcastic and cutting in return.*

> *Get your feelings hurt, and walk away sulking or crying.*

> *Blurt out, "That's disrespectful!" and administer some form of retributive punishment.*

The first response, getting angry and reviling, would only provoke your child to more anger. The second, walking away with hurt feelings and evidently upset, would teach your child that you can be manipulated by his disrespectful treatment of you. The third possible response of scolding and exacting a retributive punishment would not train your child in how to correct his disrespectful behavior. All three of the above are biblically inappropriate.

A fourth and better response eliminates the dangers of the first two and goes well beyond the traditional third reaction. This better option is to require the child to acknowledge the disrespect, ask the parent's forgiveness, and rehearse an appropriate response that reflects biblical communication in word, tone of voice and nonverbal language. The child must be able to accomplish these three components of communication in order to properly correct his behavior. Note though that this method of response does not negate the need for other forms of biblical chastisement which are appropriate to the situation.

Acknowledging Sinful Forms of Communication

The scope of this book does not allow for the development of literally scores of sinful communication forms identified in Scripture. However, I am providing an abbreviated list of twelve commonly violated principles of communication that compel parents to exact discipline.[10]

All Forms of Ungracious Speech

Let no unwholesome word proceed from your mouth, but only such (a word) as is good for edification according to the need (of the moment), that it may give grace to those who hear (Eph. 4:29).

Let your speech always be with grace, seasoned, (as it were,) with salt, so that you may know how you should respond to each person (Col. 4:6).

Disrespect

Honor your father and mother (which is the first commandment with a promise) (Eph. 6:2).

Practicing Biblical Communication

Interruption

He who gives an answer before he hears, It is folly and shame to him (Prov. 18:13).

Not Communicating

Therefore, laying aside falsehood, speak truth, each one (of you,) with his neighbor, for we are members of one another (Eph. 4:25).

Name Calling

Do not speak against one another, brethren. He who speaks against a brother, or judges his brother, speaks against the law, and judges the law; but if you judge the law, you are not a doer of the law, but a judge (of it) (James 4:11).

There is a kind of (man) who curses his father, And does not bless his mother (Prov 30:11).

Judging Motives

For I am conscious of nothing against myself, yet I am not by this acquitted; but the one who examines me is the Lord. Therefore do not go on passing judgment before the time, (but wait) until the Lord comes who will both bring to light the things hidden in the darkness and disclose the motives of (men's) hearts; and then each man's praise will come to him from God (1 Cor. 4:4-5).

Raising the Voice

A gentle answer turns away wrath, But a harsh word stirs up anger (Prov. 15:1).

Rolling the Eyes

There is a kind of (man) who curses his father, And does not bless his mother. There is a kind who is pure in his own eyes, Yet is not washed from his filthiness. There is a kind— oh how lofty are his eyes! And his eyelids are raised (in arrogance) (Prov. 30:11-13).

Manipulation

Do not answer a fool according to his folly, Lest you also be like him. Answer a fool as his folly (deserves), Lest he be wise in his own eyes (Prov. 26:4-5). (See Chapters Nine and Ten)

Sulking/Pouting

So Ahab came into his house sullen and vexed because of the word which Naboth the Jezreelite had spoken to him; for he said, "I will not give you the inheritance of my fathers." And he lay down on his bed and turned away his face and ate no food (1 King. 21:4).

An Angry Countenance

Then the Lord said to Cain, "Why are you angry? And why has your countenance fallen?" (Gen. 4:6).

Inattentiveness

A fool does not delight in understanding, But only in revealing his own mind (Prov. 18:2).

Confessing one's sin to an offended brother is not simply an option for a Christian (James 5:16, Matt. 5:21-26), it is a command that you must follow if restoration is to occur. Use of biblical terminology is important in the identification of a transgression if the child is going to "put off" the old man and "put on" the new (see Col. 3:8-10 and Eph. 4:22-25). "What I said was *disrespectful, unkind and scornful*" for example. This biblical confession will also help train the child to evaluate behavior from God's perspective rather than man's. *Which things we also speak, not in words taught by human wisdom, but in those taught by the Spirit, combining spiritual (thoughts) with spiritual (words) (1Cor. 2:13).*

Asking Forgiveness

In addition to confessing the sin to the offended parents, a child should ask forgiveness for the offense itself. Asking forgiveness is not the same thing as saying, "I'm sorry." Saying "I'm sorry" doesn't accomplish the biblical goal of putting past offenses aside. Nor does it lay the foundation to reestablish a broken trust as effectively as does asking forgiveness. When a person says "I'm sorry" the other person may respond with "I'm sorry, too," leaving the proverbial ball up in the air. Or worse, the other person may respond "You sure are sorry— you're one of the sorriest people I know!" unfairly placing the ball back in the court of the penitent Christian.

When someone asks, "Will you forgive me?", he specifically places the ball in the court of the offended brother (or parent in this case). He is saying, in effect, "Are you or aren't you going to obey God and forgive me?"(Luke 17:3 ff.).

When the parent responds with, "I forgive you", he or she is making the following commitments: "I am not going to hold this offense against you any longer, neither will I talk about it to others nor dwell on it myself." The parent is not necessarily saying, "All the trust that has been lost as a result of your sin has been restored." A Christian is commanded by God to forgive a penitent offender (Luke 17:3,4). The offending Christian has the responsibility to earn back the trust that has been lost as a result of his sin. Granting someone forgiveness, in other words, is not the same thing as declaring someone trustworthy. (See Appendix A.)

Rehearsing An Appropriate Biblical Alternative

Do you remember the initial question and the cutting disrespectful comeback at the start of this chapter? Look at it again.

Parent: "So tell me— what's new and exciting or different at school today?"

Child: "Can't you see I'm thinking? Go away and bother someone else!"

The correction, for a disrespectful response such as this one is not complete until the child practices an appropriate response to his parent's question in a way that reflects respect in all three areas of *The Communication Pie*. Therefore, the child must be trained to use the appropriate words, tone of voice, and countenance.

Choosing Appropriate Words

"The heart of the righteous studies how to answer." (Prov. 15:28)

The variety of appropriate words that could be chosen and syntactically combined to respectfully communicate any number of answers to a question, such as our example, are almost endless. I have listed a few appropriate possible responses:

▶ *"Let's see,...new and exciting or different...well, I dissected my first worm today. Yuck! It was gross!"*

▶ *"Would you believe I finally got up enough courage to ask Sandy out for lunch?"*

▶ *"If you don't mind, I'd rather talk to you about something that happened on the way home from school today."*

▶ *"I can't think of anything that was different at school today, but thank you for asking. Would you like to tell me about your day?"*

▶ *"Mom, I appreciate your asking, but right now I have something else on my mind. Do you think I could fill you in later?"*

"That's all well and good, but how do I get my child to say these things the right way? I can't put the words in his mouth now can I?"

Yes, as a matter of fact you can! However, before I explain that option, let me explain a very important biblical principle.

How to Respond to a Fool

In Chapter Three, we established that the traits of rebellious children bear a remarkable resemblance to the character traits of the proverbial fool. Keep this in mind as you read the following two verses from Proverbs 26:

"Do not answer a fool according to his folly, lest you also be like him. Answer a fool according to his folly lest, he be wise in his own eyes" (vs. 4,5).

The Bible cautions you (vs. 4) when responding to a fool (a foolish child in this case), not to answer him in the same foolish way (according to his folly) that he responds to you. Otherwise, you will be just as foolish as he. You may not, as a Christian, resort to using the same kind of disrespectful, sarcastic, manipulative, verbally abusive, foolish, or sinful form of communication that your child has wrongfully employed against you. To do so would be to stoop to his level of immaturity and prove to him that you are just as foolish (and sinful) as he is. To engage in such verbal combat would also be to allow him to manipulate you, as you will see in Chapter Nine.

The next verse, Proverbs 26:5, cautions you against something else when responding to a fool— not to let him walk away believing he is wise "lest he be wise in his own eyes." Rather, you must answer him in such a way that he realizes that he is a fool. This is best done by employing the biblical anti-manipulation techniques which will be discussed in Chapters Nine and Ten. But for now, suffice it to say that the child must understand that he has been reproved for his folly. He must know immediately that the parent is in control both of himself and of the disciplinary process. In our example he must be reproved for his disrespect and made to understand that he has a biblical responsibility to repent of his sin.

Remember that the point of The Gumnazo Principle is not just to correct a mistake. It is also to train the child to think and respond in a biblical rather than unbiblical manner. Consider the following parental responses to disrespect.

Remember, these are only suggestions that may be used verbatim or modified according to the need of the moment. With a little thought, you will likely be able to develop your own unique responses that will motivate your child to rehearse biblical alternatives upon request. It is important that the parents' tone of voice and non-verbal communication reflect grief, firmness, and gentleness rather than vengeance or sarcasm.

"That was disrespectful. Can you think of a more gracious way to answer my question or do you need to spend some time in The Think Room?" [11]

"That was inappropriate. You may try it again the right way, or there will be even more consequences than the ones I'm going to give you for being so rude."

Choosing an Appropriate Tone of Voice

Once the child has carefully selected and recited the words that convey grace and respect, he must next express those words in a tone of voice that is equally as gracious and respectful. Of course, this step must be omitted if the child's tone of voice either never was a problem or was corrected during the rewording exercise. Several attempts may be made by the child before he responds satisfactorily. If at any time during these exercises the child is stumped and truly wishes an example from his parent, he may respectfully ask for assistance with a question. For instance, he might say, "Dad, I'm not exactly sure what you're looking for. Could you please give me an example?"

On the other hand, if the child refuses to cooperate, perhaps a trip to The Think Room would be in order.

It would be easier to give examples of appropriate tones of voice if this were an audio-book. This not being the case, I suggest you and your family study the following scriptural principles and examples of appropriate forms of communication tone:

Gentle Answer: A gentle answer turns away wrath (Prov. 15:1).

Practicing Biblical Communication

Harsh Words: But a harsh word stirs up anger (Prov. 15:1).

Gentle Tongue: By forbearance a ruler may be persuaded, And a soft tongue breaks the bone (Prov. 25:15).

Sharp Reproof (or Reprimand): Now the men of Ephraim said to him, "Why have you done this to us by not calling us when you went to fight with the Midianites?" And they reprimanded him sharply (Judges 8:1, NKJV)

Fierce Words: And the men of Israel answered the men of Judah, and said, "We have ten shares in the king; therefore we also have more (right) to David than you. Why then do you despise us— were we not the first to advise bringing back our king?" Yet the words of the men of Judah were fiercer than the words of the men of Israel (2 Sam. 19:43, NKJV)

Sweetness of Speech: The wise in heart will be called discerning, And sweetness of speech increases persuasiveness (Prov. 16:21).

Gracious Speech: Let your speech always be with grace, seasoned, (as it were) with salt, so that you may know how you should respond to each person (Col. 4:6).

Pleasant Words: Pleasant words are a honeycomb, Sweet to the soul and healing to the bones (Prov. 16:24).

Rough Answer: The poor man utters supplications, But the rich man answers roughly (Prov. 18:23).

Acceptable Speech: The lips of the righteous bring forth what is acceptable, But the mouth of the wicked, what is perverted (Prov. 10:32).

At this point, you may be wondering whether or not the disrespect should be disciplined more severely than with just The Gumnazo Principle. This, of course, is a judgment call but probably the example I've used in this chapter is severe enough to require additional consequences. I do not want to leave you with the impression that Gumnazo necessarily eliminates the need for additional chastisement.

Choosing Appropriate Forms of Non-Verbal Communication

After the child rehearses an appropriate response using acceptable words and tone, he is to practice the same response using the proper non-verbal communication forms unless, of course, the non-verbal problem either did not exist or was corrected during the previous two exercises. Once again, several attempts may be necessary to achieve the desired result and the child may respectfully ask for help from the parent. It is a supplement to, not a replacement for, other biblical forms of discipline.

Appropriate non-verbal communication may be the most difficult and time-consuming piece of the pie to correct. Keep in mind that a communicator receives immediate feedback to both the words and the voice inflection he employs. That is to say he can hear what he is saying, while he is saying it. It is not always so with non-verbal communication.

When I am seated across the desk from a counselee, I know exactly what I am saying and how I am saying it.[12] What I do not know exactly, is the expression I have on my face (or my countenance as the Bible sometimes calls it.) Although I have some feedback about other non-verbal forms of my communication such as my gestures, posture and touching, I see those things from a somewhat skewed perspective and apart from the look on my face. This feedback appears to others differently than it does to me. If I had the opportunity to video-tape myself counseling (as I have had opportunity to do and to see for myself certain less than perfect non-verbal flaws in my preaching delivery), I would doubtless make some minor adjustments in my counseling delivery.

Below are a few suggested phrases to help you when correcting non-verbal communication:

▶ *"I am pleased with the words you've chosen and the manner in which you've expressed them. Now, please replace that scowl with a more pleasant expression."*

▶ *"Your words and your tone of voice are much better. Now, please say that again with a smile on your face." (Incidentally, one smile can cover a multitude of sins.)*

▶ *"Very good. Now son, I want you to sit up straight in your chair, unfold your arms, look me in the eyes, and say that exactly as you did a moment ago."*

▶ *"You are still suffering from 'poochy lip disease'. Try it again, but this time with a more cheerful countenance."*

▶ *"Uncross your legs, turn your body toward me, unfurl those eyebrows, and say that again without gritting your teeth."*

▶ *"Sweetheart, hold my hand, lean forward, smile and say..."*

▶ *"Good! Now try it again without rolling your eyes."*

"But I Don't Have The Time!"

At this point you are probably saying, "Do you realize how time consuming these exercises are? If I did this every time my kids mouth off, I could be tied up for hours every week!"

You're right. At first you may have to invest more time, effort, and thought into training your children than you currently are investing. But remember, bringing your children up "in the discipline and instruction of the Lord" (Eph. 6:4) is one of the most monumental, sacred responsibilities God has given you. You are charged by your heavenly Father to employ all the biblical resources he has provided to reproduce the character of his Son, Jesus Christ, in your children by the enabling power of the Holy Spirit. Remember as well, that the time you invest initially will end up saving you time in the long run because your children will be less and less in need of correction as they grow.

More importantly remember that the Christian character you are building in the lives of your children will have tremendous value not only throughout this life, but also throughout eternity.

"For while physical training is of some value, godliness is valuable in every way, holding promise for both the present life and the life to come" (1 Tim. 4:8).

In other words, to the degree you are investing time to produce godly character in your children, you are laying up for yourself treasure in heaven. What else are you doing with your time that is more important than this?

In this chapter, you have become acquainted with using The Gumnazo Principle in conjunction with teaching children biblical communication. We have addressed one specific communication problem faced by every parent— disrespect. The size constraints of this work will not allow for other examples, however, the gumnazo training principle can be applied to the correction of other inappropriate forms of communication. Just as your children must practice biblical communication principles to become proficient in their usage, so you, as a parent, must practice biblical discipline to become a proficient and skillful instructor.

Journaling:
A Helpful Tool for
Overcoming Anger

An instructive tool that parents can use to help their children overcome sinful anger is an *Anger Journal*. When used correctly and consistently, an Anger Journal will help children to accomplish the following:

1. *Identify the events that trigger angry responses.*
2. *Analyze and evaluate inappropriate expressions of anger.*
3. *Design alternative biblical responses to the events that trigger anger.*
4. *Improve their communication and conflict resolution skills.*
5. *Learn how to express anger without sinning.*

An Anger Journal is simply a sheet of paper on which the child, after each inappropriate expression of anger, records the answers to four specific questions:

1. *What happened that provoked me to anger?*
   (What circumstances led to my becoming angry?)
2. *What did I say and/or do when I became angry?*
   (How did I respond to the circumstances?)
3. *What does the Bible say about what I did and/or said when I became angry?*
   (What is the biblical terminology for what I did and/or said

when I became angry?)

4. *What should I have done/said when I became angry? (How could I have responded biblically when I became angry?)*

Turn for a moment to Appendix E. for a sample of how the Anger Journal should basically look, in fact the sample provided can be readily photocopied for your use. For children who are not old enough to read or write, the Anger Journal questions can be used quite effectively when articulated and discussed verbally. With slight modifications, even two or three year old children can be trained by parents who become familiar with the basic principles associated with the Anger Journal and the other journals from this book. Read Appendix B., an important supplement providing helpful guidelines and suggestions for effectively tailoring all the various journals and resources for use with your younger children.

Using the Anger Journal

I have seen this simple four-step process help many parents teach their children how to identify and correct sinful expressions of anger, and I know of at least one Christian school that is successfully using the technique with its students. You may adjust the terminology to fit your child's vocabulary as long as the basic concepts of each step remain intact.

Step 1. Identify the circumstantial provocation of the anger

Question number one— What happened that provoked me to anger? (What circumstances led to my becoming angry?) is a diagnostic question whose purpose is to help your child understand what things lead to his or her becoming angry.

The process of identifying those external circumstances which trigger an internal response of anger serves at least two purposes: First, it helps determine if your child's anger is righteous or sinful. I want to emphasize again that not all anger is sinful.

Journaling: A Helpful Tool

"God is angry with the wicked every day" (Psalm 7:11).

"He (Jesus) looked round about on them (the Pharisees) with anger" (Mark 3:5).

"Be angry (a command) and do not sin" (Eph. 4:26).

If God is sometimes angry, if Jesus was sometimes angry, and if we as believers are commanded to be angry in certain circumstances, then to say that all anger is sinful is to accuse God of wrongdoing. God designed us so that during certain periods of stress, our bodies secrete extra adrenaline which in turn produces more glucose. The additional glucose provides us with increased energy for responding to the stressful situations. This apparently is the Creator's way of biologically energizing us (when angry) to do the right things in response to anger producing circumstances.

I am indebted to David Powlison, of the Christian Counseling and Educational Foundation, who provided the idea for the following diagram. It is one of the best tools I know to help people determine whether or not their anger is sinful.

Is Your Anger Righteous or Sinful?

Righteous Anger	Sinful Anger
When God doesn't get what He wants.	When I don't get what I want.
Motivated by a sincere love for God.	Motivated by a love of some idolatrous desire.
God's will is violated.	My will is violated.
Christ is Lord of my life.	*I am the lord of my life.*
"Be angry, and do not sin." (Eph. 4:26)	"What is the source of quarrels and conflicts among you? Is not the source your pleasures that wage war in your members?" (James 4:1)

Figure 11. Determining If Anger is Righteous or Sinful

The Heart of Anger

If your anger is due to your recognition that a holy God has been offended by another's behavior, that anger is righteous. In other words, if we are angry because God's revealed will (not decreed will; for everything that happens has been foreordained by Him) is violated, our anger is righteous.

On the other hand, if your anger is the result of not having your personal desires met, that anger is usually sinful. In other words, if we are angry because someone (without sinning) prevented us from having what we really wanted, our anger is sinful. Of course, it is possible (even probable in those situations where another person's sin against God is also an offense against us) to have both righteous anger and sinful anger residing in our hearts at the same time. In such cases, you would be wise not to respond to an offender until you are certain that you have purified your motives and can speak from a more righteous motive than a selfish one. I explore the relationship between selfish motives and anger in Chapter Seven (The Heart Journal), but for now, understand that by simply identifying circumstantial evidence, it is often possible to preliminarily distinguish righteous anger from sinful anger.

Another benefit of identifying the circumstantial triggers to anger has to do with recognizing habitual response patterns. You may find that certain kinds of events trigger your angry response. Maybe there is one (or several common denominators) that, like a wrongly colored thread, runs through the entire fabric of your anger-provoking circumstances.

For example, I have recently discovered that in my own life much of what angers (frustrates) me involves time and money. This insight helped me to recognize the extent to which I was a "lover of money" (1 Tim. 6:10) and a "lover of pleasure" (2 Tim. 3:4), since it was my "spare time," time that I would normally enjoy pleasures such as fishing or hunting, which when others infringed upon caused me the most frustration.

As a review of the circumstantial anger triggers in my own life revealed a tendency to become angry over things that pertain to time and money, so a review of your child's Anger Journal may reveal those things in his life which tend to trigger anger most often. These "hot buttons," if discovered, can serve to help your child identify those things that he has idolized in his heart.

More about idols of the heart and the relationship between sinful anger will be presented in the next chapter. For now, pause and consider those things that tend to push your child's "hot button" to see if you can put your finger on what might be common denominators of provocation to sinful anger.

Step 2. Describe the outward manifestations of the anger

Question number two— What did I say and/or do when I became angry? (How did I respond to the anger-provoking circumstances?) is to help your child recall the fullness of his or her angry response. By specifying the details of an angry response, your child can see his words and actions in black and white. This exercise, in addition to being a prerequisite for a biblical diagnosis of whether or not his response was sinful, aids the child in remembering different elements of a response that is compound. That is, it can help him break such a response into bite-size pieces for a more thorough examination.

He should record his verbal responses (excluding vulgarities and profanities). With your help, he should also carefully note his tone of voice and non-verbal language. Vindictive actions such as slamming doors, hitting or throwing objects, physical assaults, clamming up, withdrawing and other retaliatory measures taken by the child should be recorded as well.

Step 3. Evaluate biblically the exact nature of the anger

Question three— What does the Bible say about what I said or did when I became angry? (What is the biblical terminology for what I said or did when I became angry?) will help your child appreciate God's perspective regarding his angry response.

A problem cannot be solved biblically until it is diagnosed using biblical terminology. Only then can you know where to look in the

Scripture for insights and direction on how to change. Only then can you choose the biblical alternatives to be put on in place of those to be put off. Usually, it is not enough just to say, "I was sinfully angry." The manifestations of sinful anger are identified with much greater specificity than that in the Bible. The following chart may be helpful in assisting your child in his evaluation. It pinpoints some common manifestations of anger using precise biblical terminology. I have subdivided this chart into two classifications of observable behavior: actions and words.

Manifestations of Anger Named

Actions

Vengeance (Rom. 12)
Striker (1 Tim. 3:3)
Hateful (Gal. 5:20)
Unkind (Eph. 4:32)
Unloving (1 Cor. 13)
Bitter (Heb. 12:15)
Wrath (Eph. 4:31)
Uncontrolled (2 Tim. 3:3)
Hurtful (Psalm 41:7)
Malice (Rom. 1:29, Eph. 4:31)
Contention (Gal. 5:20)
Spiteful (Rom. 1:30)
Pride (Rom. 1:30)
Disobedient (Rom. 1:30)
Unforgiving (Luke 17)
Unmerciful (Rom. 1:31)
Impatience (Eph. 4:2)
Intolerance (Eph. 4:2)
Ungrateful (2 Tim. 3:2)
Selfishness (1 Cor. 13:5)

Words

Disrespectful (Eph. 6:2)
Harsh words (Prov. 15:1)
Unwholesome talk (Eph. 4:29)
Cursing (James 3:9-10))
Gossip (2 Cor. 12:20)
Clamor (Eph. 4:31)
Biting & Devouring (Eph. 5:15)
Quarrelsome (1 Tim. 3:3)
Strife (Gal. 5:20)
Debate (Rom. 1:29)
Deceit (Rom. 1:29)
Whispering (Rom. 1:29)
Backbiting (Rom. 1:30)
Boasting (Rom. 1:30)
Blasphemy (2 Tim. 3:2)
False accusation (2 Tim. 3:3)
Mocking (Acts 2:13, 17:32)
Murmuring (Phil. 2:14)
Arguing (Phil. 2:13)
Vulgarity (Col. 3:8)

Figure 12. Biblical Names For Various Manifestations of Anger

Journaling: A Helpful Tool

Let me recommend that you look up and discuss each biblical reference to fully understand the meaning of each term as a part of your family devotions. The more readily your family can identify specific manifestations of anger the easier it will be for them to recognize such manifestations in their own lives.

Step 4. Develop a biblical response to the circumstantial provocation

Question four— What should I have said/done when I became angry? (How could I have responded biblically when I became angry?) is essential to the training of your child to respond to future provocations in a righteous manner.

This is perhaps the most important step in that it is the step where correction and disciplined training in righteousness (2 Tim. 3:16) can most effectively be emphasized. As your child sincerely considers various alternative biblical responses, he not only demonstrates repentance (changes his mind), but also prepares for future provocations (temptations) by exercising himself for the purpose of godliness (1 Tim. 4:7).

It is important for you to point out to your child that there are usually any number of biblically acceptable responses. I recommend that your child be encouraged to develop at least two or three alternatives for each wrong response he has recorded under step two. The more time that he spends pondering potential answers, the greater the exercise in righteousness will be.

"The heart of the wise ponders how to answer (Prov. 15:28).

The more time he spends in this step of the journal, the wiser he will become.

"The heart of the wise teaches his mouth and adds learning to his lips (Prov. 16:23).

Based on all I've said, you may have anticipated what comes next— namely, that each part of the Anger Journal is to be reviewed with your child by you (or a counselor). Having written out two or three alternative responses, I recommended that your child rehearse each response until each part of the communication pie

85

(Chapter Five) has been covered to your satisfaction.

Applications of the Anger Journal

The Anger Journal may be used in virtually any case where your child becomes angry. The following are a couple of examples:

ANGER JOURNAL (*sample 1*)

1. What circumstances led to my becoming angry?
(What happened that provoked me to anger?)

When I asked Mom if she would buy a Frisbee for me at Walmart, she said, "No" because I had not yet earned back the trust which I lost the last time she had bought me one and I threw it at my little brother when I got mad at him.

2. What did I say/do when I became angry?
(How did I respond to the circumstances?)

I raised my voice and said, "That's not fair! You never buy me anything. Daddy would have bought it for me." I then ran out to the car and left her to carry all the packages by herself.

3. What is the biblical evaluation of what I said/did when I became angry? (How does the Bible classify what I said/did when I became angry?)

Not a soft answer/grievous wounds— Prov. 15:1
Argumentative— 2 Tim. 2:24; Murmured/complained— Phil. 2:14
False accusation (lying)— Eph. 4:25 Disrespectful— Eph. 6:1-3;
Vindictive— Rom. 12:17-21 Malicious— Eph. 4:31;
Unloving, Unkind, Bad manners— I Cor. 13:5

4. What should I have said/done when I became angry?
(How could I have responded biblically when I became angry?)

1. I should have said, "Yes, Mom."
2. Said, "I don't blame you for not trusting me. I'm going to work extra hard to show you that I can be trusted with a Frisbee.
3. Offered to carry the packages to the car for her.

Journaling: A Helpful Tool

ANGER JOURNAL (*sample 2*)

1. What circumstances led to my becoming angry?
(What happened that provoked me to anger?)

I was shooting baskets in our driveway, when my Dad stuck his head out of the back door and insisted that I come in to begin doing my homework. He told my friend who was shooting with me to come back tomorrow.

2. What did I say/do when I became angry?
(How did I respond to the circumstances?)

"I don't have any homework and you're always running my friends off. It's no wonder they all think you and Mom are idiots." Then I cursed at him under my breath (but loud enough that my friend could hear) and slammed the basketball into the back door (breaking the window), & stomped off to my room sulking and pouting.

3. What is the biblical evaluation of what I said/did when I became angry? (How does the Bible classify what I said/did when I became angry?)

Lying (I did have homework and my friends don't all think my parents are idiots.) profanity, slander, backbiting, hateful.

4. What should I have said/done when I became angry?
(How could I have responded biblically when I became angry?)

Said, "OK, Dad." and explained to my friend that I really did have homework but that if I finished early I'd call him. Made an appeal: "Dad, I have new information, may I make an appeal?" (Yes) "My teacher was out sick today and the substitute teacher allowed us to catch up on some homework so I only have to study for two subjects instead of my usual four... so may I stay out and shoot baskets for another 45 minutes?" I could have appealed to Dad about changing my schedule so I would study when it isn't possible to play basketball. Appeal to Dad to install a light in the driveway so I can play basketball after dark (if I get my homework done) How about it Dad?!

Perhaps you are thinking, "I'm sure this is a very helpful tool, but the Anger Journal seems to deal only with external responses; what about helping my child to change his thoughts and his motives? Shouldn't these things be addressed as well?"

I'm glad you asked. Yes, they certainly should be addressed. In the chapters that follow, I will give you instructions that will enable you to help your child identify and change wrong thoughts and motives and replace them with appropriate biblical alternatives. But first, I must ask a more important question.

Cognitive Therapy, Behavior Modification or Christ?

What is the dynamic behind your child's ability to change— to put off the old man and put on the new man? If he is going to experience lasting change, and do so in a way that is pleasing to God, he must experience the rejuvenation of his mind by the Holy Spirit.

"...that, in reference to your former manner of life, you lay aside the old self, which is being corrupted in accordance with the lusts of deceit, and that you be renewed in the spirit of your mind, and put on the new self, which in (the likeness of) God has been created in righteousness and holiness of the truth" (Eph. 4:22-24).

His old self, with all its sinful habits must be progressively replaced by his new self. His attitude about life can and must be renewed. The resources you are learning as you read this book *do not have the ability to effectively change your child's heart apart from the Spirit's work in his life*. Your child must be a Christian in order for his mind to be rejuvenated. This is a prerequisite for his sanctification. It is not that these materials are of no use if your child is unregenerate (indeed you must train your children to be godly even before they are converted), but they will not have the internal impact upon him that they will have once he becomes a Christian.

It is not possible for a Christian to change in dependence upon his own strength. He must depend upon the Lord for the grace (the wisdom, power and desire) to live in obedience to the Bible. This is why you must faithfully proclaim the Gospel to your children. If they are lost, they must be told about the need to trust Christ's substitutionary death on the cross. If they are saved, they must be reminded that they cannot obey God apart from reliance upon the Holy Spirit's power.

Parents also must guard against viewing the materials in this book as "behavior modification" or "cognitive therapy techniques." They are biblically-derived solutions to common problems of living and are of limited value apart from the regenerating work of the Holy Spirit in your life and the life of your child.

What's at the Heart of Anger?

Let's do an experiment! That's right, you and I will conduct an experiment right here as you are reading this page. I am going to ask you to emote on command. I will count to three then ask you to produce an emotion in your heart with which you are probably well acquainted. Are you ready? Good! Sit up straight in your chair, take a deep breath, let it out slowly. Great! Now, take another breath, let it out slowly. Very good! O.K., here we go.

One, two, three... Hate! That's right! Hate Me! Come on you can do it! Hate! Hate! Hate!

What's wrong? Some of you are smiling, others are chuckling. You are supposed to be hating.

"But, Lou, it's not easy to 'womp up' a good hate. It just won't womp!"

That's right! Most of you are having great difficulty feeling hatred for a person who has done you no wrong. Had I done something to hurt you or had you perceived that I had done so, it would have been a different story. You might have thought.

"That Lou Priolo! How could he do such a thing! Doesn't he realize how wrong it was to treat me that way? He wouldn't like it if someone had done that to him. That's what I'll do. I'll do it back to him. Maybe then he'll understand how much it hurt."

If you think such thoughts, you'd probably find it much easier to hate. Why is that? Because our feelings are largely the by-products of our thoughts and actions. (If you turned your vengeful thoughts into vengeful actions, the hatred would have likely flowed even more freely). By the way, if you do not have much difficulty emoting on command, may I suggest that it is because you already have an inordinate amount of hatred in your heart for someone, and thus you have the ability to transfer such hatred to any other person with relative ease.

In chapter six, you learned how to help your child identify and conquer external manifestations of sinful anger. In this chapter and the next, you will learn how to help your child identify and conquer internal manifestations of sinful anger.

What is the Heart?

In his *Theology of Christian Counseling* [13], Dr. Jay E. Adams calls the human heart "the source or treasure-house from which the outer words and actions spring." He explains:

> In order to help us better understand the biblical meaning of heart, let us ask, "What, then, is set over against the heart, if anything?" The answer is always, without exception, the visible outer man. Worship that one gives with his lips (outer, visible, audible worship) when his heart (inner, invisible, inaudible) is far from God is a good example of this contrast (Matt. 15:8). We are instructed that man looks on the outward appearance, but (in contrast) "God looks on the heart" (1 Sam. 16:7). Without multiplying references, it is safe to say that everywhere the Bible uses the word heart to speak of the inner man (or, as Peter puts it in a thoroughly definitive way 'the hidden person of the heart.') Plainly, then, heart in the Bible is the inner life that one lives before God and himself; a life that is unknown by others because it is hidden from them.

To illustrate this contrast between the inner man (heart) and the outer man (lips, mouth, tongue, etc.), let's consider the analogy of a pitcher. (See Figure 13. on the following page.)

The reservoir part of the pitcher that holds the liquid is analogous to your heart. The spout of the pitcher is analogous to your mouth (or tongue, lips, countenance, etc.). Whatever substance is contained in the reservoir will pour out of the spout when the pitcher is appropriately tilted.

The Heart of Anger

The Lips, Mouth, and Tongue

THE HEART

Figure 13. The Biblical "Pitcher" of the Heart

If the pitcher were filled with water,
what would pour out of the spout?
If the pitcher were filled with milk,
what would pour out of the spout?
If the pitcher were filled with iced tea,
what would pour out of the spout?
If the pitcher were filled with gasoline,
what would pour out of the spout?
If the pitcher were filled with arsenic,
what would pour out of the spout?

If your child's heart is filled with foolishness,
what will pour out of his mouth? (Prov. 15:2, 12: 23)
If your child's heart is filled with deceit,
what will pour out of his mouth? (Prov. 12:20)
If his heart is filled with pride,
what will pour out of his mouth? (Ps. 101:5, 131:1)
If his heart is filled with anger,
what will pour out of his mouth? (Prov. 26:24-26)

Solomon used an analogy similiar to the pitcher when he said, ***"The mouth of fools spouts (pours out- KJV) evil things"*** ***(Prov. 15:2).*** On the other hand, if the pitcher is filled with good things, good things will pour out of the spout.

What's at the Heart of Anger?

> *If your child's heart is filled with wisdom,*
> > *what will flow out of his mouth? (Col. 3:16)*
> *If your child's heart is filled with righteousness,*
> > *what will flow out of his mouth? (Ps. 37:30, 31)*
> *If his heart is filled with virtue,*
> > *what will flow out of his mouth? (Prov. 22:11)*
> *If his heart is filled with faith,*
> > *what will flow out of his mouth? (Rom. 10:9,10)*
> *And if his heart is filled with meekness (an antidote to sinful anger), what will flow out of his mouth? (1 Peter 3:4)*

Unlike the contents of the pitcher in the above illustration, the human heart cannot be seen by man. Only God knows for sure what is inside. We can have only a glimpse into the heart by observing what pours out into words, actions, and attitudes.

"The mouth speaks out of that which fills the heart. The good man out of his good treasure brings forth what is good; and the evil man out of his evil treasure brings forth what is evil" (Matt. 12: 34b-35).

Perhaps this is why James said, *"No man can tame the tongue; it is a restless evil and full of deadly poison." (James 3:8)* The tongue is just a muscle that does what it is told to do by the heart. The tongue cannot be brought under control by a heart that is out of control. "If you have bitter jealousy and selfish ambition" (vs. 14) in your heart, what may ultimately be said by your tongue will be cursing (vs. 9-10), commotion, and every evil thing (vs. 16).

As a parent who has been commanded to bring up your children in the discipline and admonition of the Lord (Eph. 6:4), you must drive out the foolishness that is bound up in the heart of your child (Prov. 22:15), and help him replace it with the wisdom of Scripture. *"The heart of the wise teaches his mouth and adds learning to his lips." (Prov. 16:23);* Notice once again the contrast between the heart and the mouth.)

But the Bible says *"man looks at the outward appearance and only God looks at the heart" (1 Sam. 16:7).* "How can I drive out that which I cannot see?"

The Heart of Anger

Taking a Picture of the Pitcher

Good question! But remember, I said that we could get a glimpse of what is in the heart by observing "that which proceeds out of the heart" in the form of words, actions and attitudes. Although Scripture forbids us from judging what is in the heart of another (1 Cor. 4:5, James 2:4) we are permitted to ask him to judge his own thoughts and motives (Acts 5:1-4, 1 Cor. 11:28-31, 2 Cor. 13:5). Consider Proverbs 20: 5 "Counsel in the *heart* of man is as deep waters but a man of understanding will *draw* it out." (KJV)

By learning how to ask specific questions, as a parent you can draw out of your child's heart the necessary data to help him biblically diagnose any sin problem that resides therein. To the extent that you can draw the counsel out of your child's heart, you will be able to help him change not only his words, actions and attitudes, but also (and more importantly) his thoughts and motives. And this (forgive the pun), is the "heart of the matter" when it comes to helping anyone change. To the extent that you are not able to draw out the thoughts and motives of his heart, your ability to help him change at the deepest level (the only kind of change that pleases God) will be hindered. Of course, in order to make an accurate diagnosis of your child's thoughts and motives, the Scripture must be employed as the diagnostic tool.

"For the word of God is living and active and sharper than any two-edged sword, and piercing as far as the division of soul and spirit, of both joints and marrow, and able to judge the thoughts and intentions of the heart" Heb. 4:12.

The only divinely-approved diagnostic manual whereby Christians may accurately judge thoughts and motives is Scripture. Christian parent, you must learn not only how to draw the thoughts and motives out of your child, but also how to diagnose those thoughts and motives; "not in words taught by human wisdom (i.e. defense mechanism, reaction formation, love hunger, codependency, etc.), but in those taught by the Spirit (i.e. pride, blameshifting, idolatry, bondage, etc.) combining (interpreting) spiritual thoughts with spiritual words." (1 Cor. 2:13).

What's at the Heart of Anger?

Consider again the words of Henry Clay Trumbull regarding the proper diagnosis by the parent of a child's spiritual maladies:

> "No quality of a good physician is of more importance than skill in making a diagnosis of a patient's case. If a mastermind in this realm were to pass with possessiveness on the disease of every patient, the treatment of that disease would be comparatively easy. A young graduate from the medical school, or a trained nurse, would then in most instances, be capable of knowing and doing that which was liable to be misdirected, and so to be ineffective for good. As it is with the physician and his patient, so it is with the parent and his child. An accurate diagnosis is an essential prerequisite to wise and efficient treatment. The diagnosis secured, the matter of treatment is a comparatively easy matter. A parent's diagnosis of his child's case is in the discerning of his child's faults, as preliminary to a process of training for their cure. Until that is secured, there is no hope of intelligent and well-directed treatment."[14]

The goal of all this training in righteousness is to develop within your child the ability and desire to bring captive every thought to the obedience of Christ (1 Cor. 10:5). As your child learns to speak the truth in his heart (Psalm 15:2) as a matter of habit, he will gain more control over his spirit (Prov. 25:28; 16:32). In Romans 12:2 Paul explains that a Christian is totally transformed by the renewing of his mind. The process whereby this spiritual metamorphosis occurs takes place largely beneath the surface in the heart of each believer. You have not done enough if you simply teach your child simply *how to behave as a Christian*. Your responsibility as a Christian parent is to teach your child *how to think and be motivated as a Christian*, for only thereby can change in behavior be efficacious to the glory of God.

The Heart Journal

The *Heart Journal* is another valuable tool developed to train parents to draw out from their child's heart both his thoughts and motives and to help their child evaluate (judge) and correct any thoughts and motives that are unbiblical. Like the Anger Journal, the Heart Journal is a worksheet on which your child records the answers to four specific questions after each angry response:

The Heart of Anger

1. *What circumstances led to my becoming angry?*
   (What happened that provoked me to anger?)

2. *What did I say to myself (in my heart) when I became angry?*
   (What did I want, desire or long for when I became angry?)

3. *What does the Bible say about what I said to myself when I became angry?*
   (What does the Bible say about what I wanted when I became angry?)

4. *What should I have said to myself when I became angry?*
   (What should I have wanted more than my own selfish/idolatrous desire?)

(Again, see Appendix E. for a sample worksheet)

Whereas the Anger Journal is helpful in identifying and correcting *outward* manifestations of sinful anger, the Heart Journal is especially helpful in identifying and correcting *inward* manifestations of sinful anger. In other words, an honest use of the Heart Journal will train your child to do several things:
1. *Distinguish* between sinful vs. righteous anger in his heart.
2. *Identify* his sinful thoughts and motives.
3. *Alert* him to repent of unbiblical thoughts and motives associated with sinful anger.
4. *Replace* sinful thoughts and motives with those *"true, honest, just and pure" (Phil. 4:8)*, and when used in conjunction with the Anger Journal.
5. *Prevent* righteous anger from being communicated as sinful anger.

As with the Anger Journal, you may adjust the terminology of the Heart Journal to meet your child's vocabulary, provided, the basic concepts of each step are communicated accurately. Young children, who are not able to read and write, are far more able to understand and implement the basic concepts taught through the Heart Journal than most parents believe them capable of doing.

What's at the Heart of Anger?

Of course, it also takes a bit more time, effort and thought than most parents are accustomed to investing in their children's lives. (see Appendix B. for suggestions on working with your younger children to verbally employ the various journals in this book.)

Step 1: Identify the circumstances which provoked the anger

Question number one— What circumstances led to my becoming angry? (What happened that provoked me to anger?) is identical to the first question of the Anger Journal and for pretty much the same reasons. First, the answer to this question helps to determine if anger is righteous or sinful. Second, it identifies any habit patterns associated with the events that tend to trigger anger. This answer, in turn, will make it easier to recognize, and eventually dethrone, any idols which when worshipped (coveted after) produce sinful anger.

Step 2: Identify specific motives and thoughts associated with the anger

Question two— What did I say to myself (in my heart) when I became angry? (What did I want, desire or long for when I became angry?) unlike The Anger Journal the question pairs in the following three steps are not simply paraphrases of each other. The questions are similar but not synonymous. *Both* questions in each set must be answered, not either or, because each question is addressing a different issue of the heart. The first question of each set focuses on the thoughts of the heart. The second question focuses on the motives of the heart.

The ability to discern thoughts and motives when experiencing intense emotion is an essential skill for the Christian who intends to pursue holiness. Recognizing thoughts and imaginations of the heart is a prerequisite of bringing them "captive to the obedience of Christ"

The Heart of Anger

(2 Cor. 10:45, Duet. 15:9. Psalm 15:2, Isa. 55:7, Jer. 4:14, Matt. 15:19). This recognition process is made more difficult due to the following factors:

▶ *"The heart is deceitful above all things" (Jer. 17:9)* and cannot be "known" apart from the word of God which is able to *"discern (its) thoughts and motives" (Heb. 4:12).*

▶ *The heart's voice is often camouflaged by its desires.* That is, it is difficult to detect wrong thoughts because they are often based on desires which may seem legitimate when in fact they are either *wrong desires* or legitimate desires that are *desired inordinately* (James 1:12-16, 4:1,2).

▶ *The heart has the capacity to speak to itself* at the rate of over 1,200 words per minute, making such detection a bit complicated.

In answer to the first question of step two, "What did I say to myself (in my heart) when I became angry?", your child should be instructed to write out verbatim the thoughts that go through his mind at the moment of provocation. Such thoughts typically involve frequent first person references. (I, me, mine, etc.) At first, he may only be able to recognize only one or two sentences (some people also think with accompanying pictures). In time and with practice he may be able to list a half dozen or more. Here are a few common examples from our counseling files:

"That's not fair!"	"I want it and I'm going to get it!"
"I hate it when . . ."	"I can't wait to leave this place."
"I'll show her . . ."	"My parents are slave drivers."
"She's a _____!"	"I don't like it when . . ."
"She can't make me do that!"	"He doesn't love me."
"I'm not going to do it."	"Here he goes again—
"I never get to have any fun."	that same old lecture."

Emphasize the need for honest and accurate reporting. Only God and your child know whether what he tells you is correct or

98

not. Always make this clear to him. Much depends on the accuracy of the data disclosed.

Before moving on to the next question, I'd like to ask you another question. In what does your child delight? Or, to ask another way— in what does he "seek his happiness?"

"Delight yourself (seek your happiness) in the Lord and He will give you the desires of your heart." (Psalm 37:4)

God has given man the ability to delight in anything he chooses. You may delight in another person, a vocation, an avocation, an automobile, a home, travel— anything on which he sets his heart. But, is it wrong to delight in any of these things? Only if the object of such delighting is more of a delight than delighting in the Lord. To put it another way, if the object of man's delight is focused on anything other than God, the object of delight is likely an idol. Consider these two diagrams:

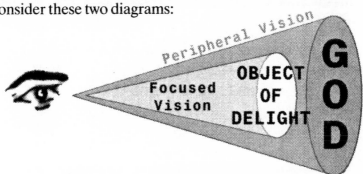

Figure 14. A Wrong Focus of Delight

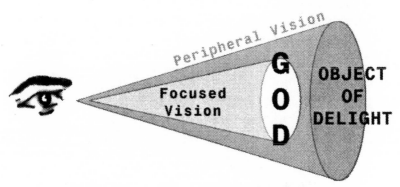

Figure 15. A Correct Focus of Delight

The Heart of Anger

If the Christian focuses his delight on the object itself, seeing God only with his peripheral vision, if at all (Figure 14.), then his focus is wrong. If, on the other hand, the Christian with his peripheral vision can see his object of delight, all the while focusing on the Gracious God who richly gives him all things to enjoy; and if he can use the object as means to praise his Creator, then he is worshipping God in his heart rather than his idol. (Figure 15.)

The answer to the second question of step two, "What did I want, desire or long for when I became angry," may be a bit more difficult to determine. Motives (passions, desires and affections, etc.) are not always as readily available to awareness as are thoughts. It is often not until you stop and ask yourself specific questions concerning these things that you can put your finger on what they are. If your child has difficulty identifying his motives by asking this question on the Heart Journal, have him try some of these questions:

> *What is it that I believe I can't be happy without?*
> *What is it that I crave?*
> *What is it that I believe I must have?*
> *What do I spend most of my spare time thinking about?*
> *What is it that I worry most about losing?*
> *What do I delight in (seek my happiness) the most?*
> *What do I love more than I love God and my neighbor?*

When introducing the Heart Journal to a new counselee at the counseling center, I typically have him answer only the first two sets of questions on his own. Then I show him how to answer questions three and four in the following counseling session. I suggest that you follow a similar pattern with your child when introducing him to the Heart Journal. Ask him to write out the answers to questions one and two on his own. Then, sometime later on that day (or perhaps as a part of his quiet time the following day) work with him in answering questions three and four (via the aforementioned Gumnazo Principle) until he becomes adept at answering the questions himself.

What's at the Heart of Anger?

Here are some common childhood desires. The first group are desires which are inherently wrong. The second group are desires which, although not inherently wrong, may be desired too intently by your child.

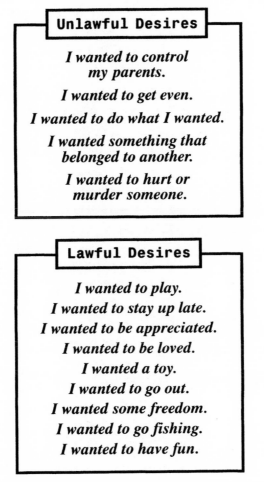

Unlawful Desires

I wanted to control my parents.

I wanted to get even.

I wanted to do what I wanted.

I wanted something that belonged to another.

I wanted to hurt or murder someone.

Lawful Desires

I wanted to play.
I wanted to stay up late.
I wanted to be appreciated.
I wanted to be loved.
I wanted a toy.
I wanted to go out.
I wanted some freedom.
I wanted to go fishing.
I wanted to have fun.

If you are going to help your child identify and dethrone any idols in his heart, you must first be certain that he can distinguish those desires which are sinful in and of themselves from those which are not. Of course this means that you both will have to become more familiar with certain Scripture passages than you probably are presently.

Getting Anger
Problems Right

Allow me to say it again—

> A problem cannot be solved biblically until it is diagnosed using biblical terminology. Only then can you know where to look in Scripture for insights and direction to change. Only then can you identify the biblical alternatives which are to be put on in place of those which are to be put off.

Teaching your child not only to identify the thoughts and motives of his angry heart, but also to evaluate (discern) them according to Scripture (Heb. 4:12), is foundational to teaching him how to make them *"captive to the obedience of Christ" (1 Cor. 10:5)*. The diagnoses should again be made *"not using the words that man's wisdom teaches, but that which the Holy Spirit teaches comparing (interpreting) spiritual thoughts with spiritual words" (1 Cor. 2:17)*. The practice of familiarizing himself with the terminology of Scripture combined with the exercise of writing down the appropriate diagnoses should, over time, build biblical discernment into his heart as he develops a mature conscience— *"But strong meat belongs to those who are mature, even to those whose senses have been exercised to discern between good and evil" (Heb. 5:14)*.

The third and fourth steps of the Heart Journal are practical exercises to "exercise" a child's spiritual senses that he might mature in Christ knowing the difference between good and evil:

Step 3. Evaluate the nature of anger producing thoughts and motives biblically

Question number three of the Heart Journal— What does the Bible say about what I said to myself when I became angry? (What does the Bible say about what I wanted when I became angry?

When training your child to answer this question, encourage him to think in terms of identifying specific sins (unless of course his thoughts were not sinful).

Let us say, for example, in response to not being allowed to visit with a close friend due to prior family commitments, your child thinks the following:

1. *"That's not fair."*
2. *"My mother never lets me do what I want to do."*
3. *"She doesn't want me to have any fun."*
4. *"She's a selfish, contentious shrew."*
5. *"I can't wait to get out of here."*

Using the Heart Journal, you would then evaluate each thought using the biblical terminology that best describes the sins associated with the thought:

1. *"That's not fair."*—
   False accusation / bad theology. Even God is not "fair"— He is just. My mother has not been unjust in her dealing with me. (Phil. 4:8, 2 Tim. 3:2,3). (I recommend that after each evaluation an appropriate Scripture reference be cited.)
   Irresponsibility / selfishness. I should be more concerned about keeping my promises than having fun (Ps. 15:4).

2. *"My mother never lets me do what I want to do."*—
   Dishonesty. She doesn't always keep me from doing what I want to do (Phil. 4:8).
   Selfishness. What I wanted to do is not as important as hon-

oring my mother (1 Cor. 13:5, Eph. 6:2).

3. *"She doesn't want me to have any fun."*—

Judging motives. I don't know what she wants because I cannot read her mind and she has not told me what she wanted. (1 Cor. 4:5).

Unloving. Love believes that which is best about another. I should, therefore, put the best possible interpretation on her actions. (1 Cor. 13:7).

4. *"She's a selfish, contentious shrew."*—

False accusation / dishonesty. It is certainly possible that her motives are unselfish and that she has what she believes is a good reason to keep me from seeing my friend.

Name calling/evil speaking. There is not enough evidence to convict her of being selfish or contentious. A shrew is not a name that God uses to classify people and I, therefore, should not use it (1 Cor. 2:13, James 4:11).

5. *"I can't wait to get out of here."*—

Impatience. The Lord has placed me in this family for His purposes. It is for Him to decide when I leave (Eph. 4:2).

Ungratefulness. I should be focusing on what my parents have already given me rather than on what I wish they would have given me (1 Thes. 5:18).

I have included in Appendix C. a chart that will make it easier for you and your child to identify some of the most common anger-related sinful thought patterns. The chart is not exhaustive but may be expanded and "personalized" by you and your child as you spend more time studying God's word for additional biblical categories of wrong thinking.

The second question in step three, "What does the Bible say about what I wanted when I became angry?" is used to evaluate (classify) our motives as either wrong or right.

Getting Anger Problems Right

If the desire is sinful, the evaluation is relatively simple.

Motive	Biblical Evaluation
I wanted to get even	Revenge
I wanted to look at pornography	Lust
I wanted to kill him	Murder
I wanted to trick him	Deception
I did not want to obey my parents	Disobedience
I did not want to share my toys	Selfishness

If, however, the desire is not inherently sinful, the question then becomes, "Did I want something that God says is good too much, or did I want some good thing so much that I was willing either to sin in order to get it (by getting angry) or to sin because I couldn't have it (again by getting angry?)

What is the Source of Sinful Anger?

The book of James was possibly the first New Testament book that was written. The Christians to whom the Lord's brother was writing were having such conflicts with each other that James used the words *wars and fightings* to describe the outward manifestation of their anger. In the beginning of chapter four, the question he asks cuts right through such outward manifestations and focuses on the internal causes or motives of the anger. "What is the *source* of quarrels (wars- KJV) and conflicts (fighting- KJV) among you?" (James 4:1) He then answers his own question to reveal to the readers exactly what is at the heart of their angry disputes (or what is in their heart that produced their angry disputes.) "Is not the source (of these quarrels and conflicts) the *pleasures* that wage war in your members?" Yes! Is the intended reply.

We have angry conflicts with one another because our pleasures (desires which are not necessarily sinful in and of themselves) have become so intense that they are at war within our members. The term to *"wage war"* is a word that has as its root the idea of being "encamped." When our desires (as good as they may be) become so strong that they *"camp out"* in our hearts, those desires (as good as they may be) become sinful, idolatrous desires; not because they are sinful desires in themselves, but because they are desired *inordinately*. Our hearts covet them so intensely that we are willing to sin (war and fight) either in order to obtain them or because we are not able to obtain them.

James, in chapter four, continues to focus on the Christians' motives by unpacking in more detail what he has just said.

"You lust (a different word that also implies a desire for something that is not inherently sinful) *and do not have, so you commit murder"* (a biblical effigy for and manifestation of hatred, see Matt. 5:21,22, 1 John 3:15). *"And you are envious* (another synonym for desire with an implication of coveting which is sometimes associated with anger) *(Acts 7:9, 17:5), and cannot obtain: so you fight and quarrel* (verbal forms of the words fightings and quarrels in verse one, which mean to strive or dispute and to contend or quarrel respectively.)

Having broken down into its component parts verse one, James continues to press home his point that the cause of their relationship problems is their selfish idolatrous motives as evidenced by their self-centered prayer life.

"You do not have because you do not ask. You ask and do not receive because you ask with wrong motives so that you may spend it on your pleasures (the same word for pleasure that was used in verse one from which our English word for hedonism is derived). *You adulteresses* (their selfish motives have not only hurt their interpersonal relationships with each other, but have so affected their relationship with God that he views them as unfaithful spouses), *do you not know that the friendship with the world* (the love of the world to the point of idolatry) *is hostility toward God?* (They have loved the world to such a degree that the love of God is not in them (1 Jn 2:15), again demonstrating that their own desires are affecting their relationship not only with each other but also with God.) *Therefore whoever wishes to be a friend of the world makes himself an enemy of God."*

On the other hand, God desires us to desire Him with the same kind of desire with which He desires us. *"Or do you think that the Scripture speaks to no purpose: 'He jealously desires the Spirit which He has made to dwell in us?'"* The Spirit of God earnestly desires that we not displace our love for Him with a love for anything that the world has to offer.

The best evidence that a Christian desires (loves) something more than he desires (loves) God, is his willingness to sin against God, either *in order to acquire that desire or because he cannot acquire it. "If ye love Me keep My commandments," Jesus said (John 14:15).* One of the most common sins that demonstrates the presence of inordinate desire is anger. By having an angry child identify biblically the kind of sin that is associated with his anger, a parent can help him correct his anger not simply *externally* (i.e. temper tantrums, sarcasm, fighting, etc.) but *internally* (idolatry: love of pleasure, love of money, love of praise, etc.) in his foolish heart, where the anger resides.

Both James and John identified loving the world as idolatry (James 4:4, 1 John 2:15). For identifying specific kinds of idolatry, you may find it helpful to consider those things that the Scriptures indicate a person may love or desire or delight in too much.

For example, let's consider four of the most common idols: love of money, love of pleasure, love of approval, and love of power.[16]

The Love Of Money

"But those who <u>want</u> to get rich fall into temptation and a snare and <u>many foolish and harmful desires</u> which plunge men into ruin and destruction. For <u>the love of money</u> is a root of all sorts of evil, and some <u>by longing for it</u> have wandered away from the faith, and pierced themselves with many a pang" (1 Tim. 6:9,10 emphasis added).

The love of money is *a* root, not *the* root as the KJV translators inprecisely translated (the anartherous noun). It is one of *several* root desires identified by the Bible which men long for (covet or desire excessively) to their own harm.

Children may demonstrate a love of money by hoarding money

in their piggy banks or by constantly asking parents for cash. I've counseled many children who would even steal money from their parents, by taking money from their mother's purse or their father's wallet.

The Love Of Pleasure

"He who loves pleasure will be a poor man. He who loves wine and oil will not become rich" (Prov. 21:17 emphasis added).

"But realize this, that in the last days difficult times will come. For men will be lovers of self, lovers of money... lovers of pleasure rather than lovers of God" (2 Tim. 3:1,2,4).

The ability to enjoy pleasure is a blessing from God who "richly supplies us all things to enjoy" (1 Tim. 6:17). The setting of one's heart on pleasure to the point of hedonism (taken from the same Greek word for pleasure), so that one becomes "enslaved to various lusts and pleasures" (Titus 3:3), is a heart problem of which sinful anger is a symptom.

When children refuse to quit their fun activities at the request of mom or dad, or become excessively sorrowful when it is time to turn off the television or computer game, or whine and complain that there is no one to play with, it is likely that they are, at least momentarily, loving pleasure more than they are loving God.

The Love Of Approval

"For they (the Pharisees) loved the approval of men rather than the approval of God" (John 12:43 emphasis added).

"But they (the scribes and the Pharisees) do all their deeds to be noticed by men, for they broaden their phylacteries and lengthen the tassels of their garments and they love the place of honor at banquets and the chief seats in the synagogues, and respectful greetings in the market places, and being called by men, Rabbi" (Matt. 23:5-7 emphasis added).

To desire the approval of others is not necessarily wrong. If it were, to praise or commend your child would be to tempt him to sin. But, as with money and pleasure (and anything else that is not inherently evil), to desire approval so much that it turns into the love of approval is wrong. The scribes and the Pharisees (like so many today and down through the ages) *were approval addicts.* That is, their desire for approval was so inordinate that they were in bondage to it. *"For by what a man is overcome, by this he is enslaved" (2 Peter 2:19).* They wanted approval so much that they spent much of their time and effort doing those things that would bring glory from men. Even those things that were religious in nature (like prayer and fasting and giving) were done by some with a motive to gain man's approval, for which Jesus said, *"They have their reward in full" (Matt. 6:2).*

When children are taught before they are teenagers to desire the approval of God more than the approval of man, the problem of peer pressure can be eliminated.

I believe that the love of approval is at the heart of giving into peer pressure. Children who dress and adorn themselves contrary to the guidelines established by their parents are more than likely struggling with a greater desire to please men than to please God. The same love of approval motive may manifest itself in the music they listen to, the recreational activities they enjoy and the language they use.

The Love Of Power (Control)

"I wrote something to the church; but Diotrophes, <u>who loves to be first among them,</u> does not accept what we say. For this reason, if I come, I will call attention to his deeds which he does, unjustly accusing us with wicked words; and not satisfied with this, <u>neither does he himself receive the brethren, and he forbids those who desire to do so, and puts them out of the church."</u> (3 John 9 emphasis added).

Diotrophes loved to hold the highest rank among the leaders in church. His love for preeminence turned him into a tyrannical leader who was even threatened by a visit from others who might disagree with him. Once again, to have a desire to manage those things over which the Lord has given you responsibility is not a sin.

When, however, that desire to manage is turned into "lording it over those allotted to your charge" (1 Peter 5:3), that proper desire has turned into an idolatrous love of power.

Therefore, children who continually refuse to submit to parental authority, or who are adept at manipulating their parents, (see chapters nine and ten) or who bully their siblings and friends, might be doing so out of a motive that is set on controlling those things over which God has not given them authority.

Recall the thoughts recorded in the Heart Journal we were considering:

"That's not fair..."
"My mother never lets me do what I want to do."
"She doesn't want me to have any fun."
"She's a selfish contentious shrew."
"I can't wait to get out of here."

Can you identify some possible wrong motives (idolatrous desires) out of which these thoughts might flow? Of course, only the child, whose heart produced these wrong thoughts, can truly evaluate any wrong motive, but here is one possibility:

Wrong Motives

That's not fair...	*Love of Control*
She never lets me do what I want...	*(Desire to usurp*
I can't wait to get out of here...	*parental authority)*
Mother never let's me do what I want...	*Love of Pleasure*
She doesn't want me to have any fun...	
She's a selfish contentious shrew...	*Desire for Revenge*

As you familiarize yourself and your child with those things that the Bible specifically identifies as idolatrous as well as with those things that he desires to the point of anger, you both will become more proficient at using God's word as the discerner of the thoughts and intents of your hearts.

Step 4: Develop alternative biblical thoughts and motives to replace the unbiblical ones

Question four— What should I have said to myself when I became angry? (and What should I have wanted more than my own selfish desires?)

It is not enough to identify and remove (put off) wrong thoughts and motives from the heart. In order for change to be biblical (effective, enduring, and pleasing to God), the Christian must replace sinful thoughts and motives with (put on) righteous ones. He must make it his goal to do the following:

▶ *To be pure in heart (Matt 5:8)*
▶ *To speak the truth in his heart (Ps. 15:2)*
▶ *To desire truth in all his innermost being (Ps. 51:6)*
▶ *To let his mind think on whatever is true, honorable, just, pure, of good repute, excellent, and worthy of praise (Phil. 4:8)*
▶ *To renew his mind (Rom. 12:2)*
▶ *To be renewed in the spirit of his mind (Eph. 4:23)*
▶ *To gird up his loins with truth (Eph. 6:14)*

This is by far the most important step of the Journal because it is where repentance (change of mind) is brought to fruition. It is where the "correction and disciplined training in righteousness" (2 Tim. 3:17) most concretely takes place. It is the part of the training, The Gumnazo Principle, that best prepares your child for dealing with future provocation and temptations biblically. By identifying and rehearsing biblical alternatives to the sinful thoughts and motives of a heart that has to some extent been trained in covetous practices (2 Peter 2:14), your child can retrain himself to covet those things that are lawful.

In response to the question, "What should I have said to myself when I became angry," the child should be encouraged to record as many biblically accurate alternative thoughts as he can in a reasonable amount of time (10-15 minutes at first). These alternatives should reflect firstly— theological accuracy (especially focusing on God's sovereignty as it relates to His ability to have prevented the provocation from occurring), secondly, Biblical hope (especially as it relates to His working all things together for the good of the believer who has been predestined to be conformed to the image of Christ), and thirdly, the putting on of those antithetical concepts to anger identified in Scripture (gentleness, contentment, kindness, tenderheartedness, forgiveness, etc.). You may choose to help him shape and articulate his answers.

As an alternative to thinking *"That's not fair!"*, the child might consider such possible alternatives as the following:

"Lord, I know that you could have prevented this apparent injustice, but I realize that You have a purpose in it. Please help me respond to this trial in such a way that it will make me more like Christ." *or*

"There really is not enough evidence to convict my mother of being unfair. I better not answer a matter before I hear it" (Prov. 18:13). *or*

"Did I do anything to cause my mother to respond this way?" *or*

"Fair or not, I've got to respond to my mother with gentleness and respect. I'd better ask the Lord for wisdom." *or*

"Life is not always fair but God is always just. I need to commit my case 'to Him who judges rightly.'"

To replace the thought, *"My mother never let's me do what I want"*, consider the following options:

"What the Lord wants is more important than what I want." *or*

"Perhaps He wants me to do something else right now." *or*

"If I cannot respectfully persuade her to change her mind by making a biblical appeal, I will have to conclude this is not what the Lord wants. Now, how shall I make that appeal?" *or*

"'Never' is not quite true; it seems that she does tend to not give me what I want as much as I would like, but I'd better collect more data before I even think of talking to her about that." *or*

"If I want to do what I want to do so much that I sin because my mother (not to mention God Himself) will not allow me to do it, then what I want to do, I want too much."

Getting Anger Problems Right

Rather than, *"She doesn't want me to have any fun"*, perhaps these thoughts would do:

"Since she hasn't told me what her motives are in this case, and since I cannot read her mind, I'd better assume the best." *or*
"God is probably more concerned with my using this trial as an opportunity to grow as a Christian than He is my having fun." *or*
"God has given me more to do in life than just having fun." *or*
"Having fun is only important as it relates to living my entire life to the glory of God (it is a means to an end, not an end in and of itself)." *or*
" Sometimes I want to have fun too much."

Instead of *"She's a selfish contentious shrew"*, how about these thoughts:
"She's my mother and God expects me to honor her." *or*
" I cannot honor her by calling her unbiblical names." *or*
"I've been acting selfishly because I can't get my own way." *or*
"What I should do is thank her for what she has done and is doing for me and praise her for her good qualities (just as the children of the Proverbs 31 woman rise up and call her blessed)."

Rather than *"I can't wait to get out of here"*, perhaps your child could respond as follows:

"I need endurance so that after I have done the will of God I may inherit the promise." *or*

"Lord, forgive me for being impatient and help me to be content." *or*

"I can do all things through Christ who strengthens me." *or*

"My parents are divinely appointed agents through which God has determined to conform me into the image of Christ." *or*

"If I do not learn what the Lord wants me to learn when I am in this circumstance, He will likely raise up similar or worse circumstances when I do get out of here to teach me what I have not learned." *or*

"My stay in this home is only temporary. God says I must leave someday. I will be patient while I am here and thankful for the opportunity to grow while I am here. I will focus my attention on how I can minister to my parents and please them as long as I am under their authority."

"It Will Never Work With My Child!"

By this time some of you probably are saying, "Is he kidding? My kid doesn't know the Bible well enough to think those kinds of thoughts, neither does he seem to have any desire to do so. It will never work with my child."

First, I am not kidding. God commands you to train your child to think and act like a Christian. Second, using the Heart Journal in the prescribed manner will not only help train your child to think and act like a Christian but also will better aquaint him with God's Word as he turns to Scripture (with your help at first) to identify, diagnose and correct sinful thoughts and motives. Third, concerning their desire, it is God who works in your believing children to make them willing to do His good pleasure (Phil. 2:13).

In addition, since the Heart Journal specifically deals with motives, it can be used to identify, diagnose and correct such lack of desire to bring every thought captive to the obedience of Christ. Finally, please remember, dear parent, that you are neither a prophet, nor the son or daughter of a prophet (Amos 7:14), and therefore, ought not to make such unbiblical predictions as "It will never work with my child." Especially since what you are prophesying is contrary to our Lord's command. Perhaps you should consider doing a few Heart Journals of your own to correct any unbiblical thoughts and motives in your heart.

Inculcating Godly Motives in Your Child

The last question on the Heart Journal is the question: "What should I have wanted more than my own selfish desires?"

The ultimate answer to this question in every case ought to be to glorify God. This concept may be expressed in a variety of ways.

Getting Anger Problems Right

Before identifying some of the forms of motivation that glorify God, consider some of those delights, loves, and longings that Scripture encourages the believer to develop. (Incidentally, it could be suggested that a child who lacks at least some of these desires might not be a Christian at all, and therefore ought to be encouraged to examine himself to see whether he is truly in the faith; cf. 2 Cor. 13:5).

A Christian's first love should be love for the Lord his God that exudes from his heart, mind, soul, and strength (Luke 10:27). This ought to be the supreme motive for everything that a Christian does. He may have in his heart good and noble motives in addition, but this love must be preeminent.

A Christian's motive should be to love his neighbor as (with the same intensity) he loves himself. As every man naturally "nourishes and cherishes himself" so the Christian is to love his neighbor to the same degree (Luke 10:27).

Using these two righteous loves, we may categorize the other lawful loves spoken of by name in the Bible. These of course are lawful to the degree that they are subordinate to loving God. Here is a partial list:

Lawful Loves

The Love of the Word of God	*Psalm 119:140*
The Love of Wisdom	*Proverbs 4:6, 8:17*
The Love of Mercy	*Micah 6:8*
The Love of Truth	*2 Thes. 2:10*
The Love of Peace	*Zec. 8:19*
The Love of (that which is) Good	*Amos 5:15*
The Love of the Lord's return	*2 Tim. 4:8*
The Love of Life (not his own)	*1 Peter 3:10*
The Love of Light	*John 3:19*
The Love of One's Spouse	*Ephesians 5:25*

By training your child how to answer this final question in the Heart Journal, you will be training him to develop proper motivation and training him to set his affections on the things above rather than on the things that are on earth (Col. 3:2).

When Peter rebuked the Lord after hearing His prophecy concerning His impending (immanent) suffering, he was rebuked—

"You are __not setting your mind on God's interests__, but man's" *(Matt. 16:23, emphasis added).*

Paul contrasts the "enemies of the cross of Christ, whose end is destruction, whose God is their appetite, whose glory is their shame, and who set their minds on earthly things," with those genuine believers whose "citizenship is in heaven" and who eagerly wait for a Savior, the Lord Jesus Christ (Phil 3:18-20).

In answering this last question, your child will identify those desires which he ought to delight in, love, pursue, set his affection on, covet, etc. He will be using the *"momentary light affliction"* to *"produce an eternal weight of glory far beyond all comparison"* as with the eyes of his heart he learns to *"look not at the temporal things which are seen, but at the eternal things which are not seen"* *(2 Cor. 4:17,18).*

In every situation that once brought sinful anger to his heart as a result of delighting too much in some temporal pleasure, your child can learn to increasingly delight in doing God's revealed will.

"I delight to do thy will, O my God, thy law is within my heart" *(Ps. 40:8).*

Rather than asking himself, "What do I want to do?" The child can be trained to ask the Lord, "What do You want me to do?"

What then are some alternative biblical motives (desires) for your child to develop when he discovers idolatrous ones in his heart? How can the desires to love and glorify and obey God be expressed so that they may prayerfully be cultivated to maturity? What are the right answers to the question, "What should I have wanted more than my own selfish desires?" At the top of the following page I have listed a number to get you started thinking in this direction. Next to each response I've suggested a portion of Scripture to be memorized in order to assist the cultivation of each of these godly motives.

Righteous Desires

To love and glorify God by ...	**Matt. 5:16**
To delight in doing God's will which was ...	**Psalm 40:8**
To be more like Jesus Christ in this way:...	**2 Cor. 3:18**
To love my neighbor as myself.	**Matt. 22:34-40**
To have wisdom and understanding.	**Prov. 4:5-9**
To honor and obey my parents.	**Eph. 6:1-3**
To delight in God's Word.	**Psalm 1:2**
To delight more in giving than receiving.	**Acts 20:35**
To minister to others.	**Matt. 20:25-28**
To offer a blessing.	**1 Pet. 3:8-16**
To show my parents that I am trustworthy.	**Prov. 20:6**

Going back to our original example of a child complaining about not being allowed to visit a friend due to prior commitments, let's take another look at the thoughts which were analyzed for potential wrong desires along with their corresponding biblically adjusted thoughts—

Original Thoughts
That's not fair...
She never lets me do what I want...
I can't wait to get out of here...

Original Desires
Love of Control
(Desire to usurp
parental authority)

vs.

Appropriate Thoughts
"Life is not always fair, but God is always just."
"I need to commit myself to Him who judges righteously."
"What the Lord wants is more important than what I want. Perhaps He wants me to do something else right now."
"My parents are divinely appointed instruments through which God has determined to conform me to the image of Christ."

Appropriate Desires
To delight in doing God's will.
To be more like Jesus Christ.
To honor and obey my parents.
To control only those things which I am biblically responsible to control and to trust Sovereign God to work all things together for good (especially those which I cannot control).

The Heart of Anger

Original Thoughts
"She never lets me do what I want"
"She doesn't want me to have fun."

Original Desires
Love of Pleasure

VS.

Appropriate Thoughts
"What the Lord wants is more important than what I want. If I want to do something so much that I sin because my my mother (and God) forbids it, then what I want to do , I want to do too much."

"Having fun is only important when it relates to living my entire life to the glory of God. It is a means to an end but not the end itself."

"God is more interested in my growing as a Christian through this trial than in my having fun."

Appropriate Desires
To know Christ, the power of His resurrection, the fellowship of His suffering...

To be holy more than to be unhappy.

To be conformed to the image of Christ (which will bring me lasting happiness and pleasure).

Original Thoughts
"She's a selfish, contentious shrew."

Original Desires
Revenge or Malice

VS.

Appropriate Thoughts
"She's my mother and God expects me to honor her. I cannot honor her by calling her sinfully disrespectful names. What I should be doing is blessing her, thanking her for what she has done and is doing for me and I shoud be praising her for her good qualities.

Appropriate Desires
To honor my parents.
To glorify God.
To bless others.
To do good and to be good.

To conclude this chapter, here are two Heart Journals which parallel the two scenarios used to complete the Anger Journals in Chapter Eight. Remember that these are only examples and are not uniquely correct. Any variety of possible answers exist which are just as (if not more) correct.

Getting Anger Problems Right

HEART JOURNAL (*sample 1*)

1. What happened that provoked me to anger?
(What are the circumstances that led to my becoming angry?)

I was shooting baskets in our driveway when my dad stuck his head out of the back door and insisted that I come in to begin my homework. He told my friend who was shooting with me to come back tomorrow.

2. What did I say to myself (in my heart) when I became angry?
(What did I want, desire or long for when I became angry?)

I'm right in the middle of a game. I can't believe he's spoiling my fun. I hate it when he does that. He's always running my friends off. It's my life! Why doesn't he let me do what I want to do? (I wanted to finish playing basketball with my friends. I wanted to have fun. I wanted to decide when I should play and when I should do my homework.)

3. What does the Bible say about what I said to myself when I became angry? (What does the Bible say about what I wanted?)

The Bible says my thoughts were sinful: Selfish, Hateful, Dishonest, Rebellious (The Bible says my desires were idolatrous since I was a "lover of pleasure" more than a "lover of God". Also, since I desired to "control" what He did not give me the responsibility to control, I "loved to be in control" more than I loved Him.)

4. What should I have said to myself when I became angry? (What should I have wanted more than my own selfish and idolatrous desire?)

I could have said to myself, "I'm right in the middle of a game. Perhaps I can appeal to Dad to let me finish the game before I start my homework. If not, I'll have to assume the Lord has other plans for my time. One thing is sure— my having fun is not as important to God as is honoring my father. It will be nice when my father trusts me to keep my own schedule and to make my own decisions. The more I obey him, the more likely he will be to trust me." (I should have desired to love God

119

more than loving the pleasure of playing basketball. I should have desired to be more Christ-like and submit to my father's will than to have sinfully imposed my will on his.)

HEART JOURNAL (sample 2)

1. What happened to provoke me to anger?
(What were the circumstances that led to my becoming angry?)

Mom said "no" when I asked her if she would buy this Frisbee for me that was on sale at Wal-Mart. She said that the last time she had bought me one, I used it to throw at my little brother when I got mad at him.

2. What did I say to myself (in my heart) when I became angry?
(What did I want, desire or long for when I became angry?)

I'm the best Frisbee thrower in town. I've got to have that Frisbee so I can show my friends how good I am. She'll never trust me with anything ever again. I'll make her pay by leaving her to carry the packages to the car by herself. (I wanted the Frisbee so that I could have fun and show off to my friends.)

3. What does the Bible say about what I said to myself when I became angry? (What does the Bible say about what I wanted?)

The Bible says my thoughts were proud, vindictive, rash, boastful, unloving and presumptuous. (The Bible says that my desires were idolatrous in that I was a "lover of pleasure" more than a "lover of God", and I "loved the approval of man" more than the approval of God.)

4. What should I have said to myself when I became angry?
(What should I have wanted more than my own selfish and idolatrous desire?)

I guess the Lord doesn't want me to have this Frisbee right now. Perhaps the Lord knows that if I had it now I would be tempted to use it to gain approval rather than to glorify Him. When I can demonstrate over time that I can control my anger my mother will likely let me have one. Rather than throw my usual temper tantrum, I'm going to bless Mom by helping her carry the packages to the car.

Disrespect and Manipulation

In counseling parents of angry children, I give the following test to determine just how manipulative a child might be. To take the test yourself, use the rating scale below to respond to the statements listed, rating each as to the frequency they occur.

Rating Scale

Never or hardly ever *5*

Seldom *4*

Occasionally *3*

Frequently *2*

Almost always *1*

Always *0*

Manipulation Test

____ 1. I have to repeat and/or reword instructions before my child follows them.

____ 2. When I ask my child to do something, he asks me, "Why?"

Disrespect and Manipulation

___ 3. I find myself having to justify my decisions to my child.

___ 4. I have grown weary of certain "topics" which seem to be discussed over and over again with my child.

___ 5. I walk away from discussions with my child and I feel guilty.

___ 6. My child lies to me.

___ 7. My child is disciplined almost entirely by one parent.

___ 8. I rescind disciplinary actions (or lift restrictions) because of appeals by my child.

___ 9. I find myself defending my positions to my child.

___ 10. I get frustrated because my child seems beyond my control.

___ 11. I get sidetracked by my child's clever distractions when I attempt to discipline him.

___ 12. My child tries to obligate me to behave a certain way by telling me what I should, ought to, or must do (other than for biblical reasons).

___ 13. When my child wants something from me, he tries to motivate me to give it to him without telling me directly what he wants.

___ 14. My child is able to procrastinate by cleverly using various stall tactics when I assign him a responsibility.

___ 15. My child is able to play on my emotions in order to get what he wants.

___ 16. I hesitate to say "no" to my child out of fear of what he might do.

___ 17. I am unsuccessful at completing the intended instruction and discipline of my child due to his unwillingness to cooperate.

___ 18. My child is so tenacious in wanting his own way that I either give in to his desires or give up on trying to train him.

___ 19. My child continues to beg and plead to have his way after I've denied his appeal the first time.

___ 20. My child is more disobedient and disrespectful in front of others than he is when he knows that such behavior is not likely to embarrass me.

_____ Total Score

Scoring Your Test

Add up the total number of points to determine your score. Based on 100%, if your total score is 90 or better, you are probably quite adept at preventing manipulation by your child. If your total score is between 75 and 90, you are probably being manipulated to a relatively small degree. If your total score is below 75, it is likely that you are being manipulated to a great extent. The lower your score, the greater your effort should be in learning and applying the principles in this chapter.

Disrespect, Manipulation and Anger

Do you know how disrespect and manipulation are related to anger? The very same lusts which tempt you to become sinfully angry when you do not get your way, tempt you to employ sinful means to obtain what you want. *"Each one is tempted when he is carried away and enticed by his own lust"(James 1:14).* An idolatrous lust, you remember, is something you want so much that you are either willing to sin in order to get it, or sin because you can't have it. For many, unholy anger is the sin we commit when we can't have what we want. Manipulation and disrespect are two common sins that many will resort to in order to get what they inordinately desire.

Disrespect and Manipulation

What is Manipulation?

To manipulate is to attempt to control. For a Christian, manipulation is using unbiblical means of controlling or influencing another person. More specifically, it is often an attempt to gain control of another individual or situation by inciting an emotional reaction rather than a biblical response from that individual. In Luke chapter ten, for example, Martha "was distracted with all her preparations and she came up to Him (Jesus) and said, 'Lord, do you not care that my sister has left me to do all the serving alone? Then tell her to help me.'"

Martha wanted, perhaps too much, assistance with her food preparations and was frustrated that her sister left her to do all the serving by herself. Rather than telling the Lord exactly what she wanted (help with the cooking), she attempted to play on His emotions (sympathy and perhaps guilt). "Do you not care?" Another element of manipulation can be seen in Martha's response. Here she was attempting to motivate someone to fulfill her personal desires (there's that word again) without clearly stating them. An appeal for sympathy, rightly expressed, is not necessarily wrong as long as the true desire behind such an appeal is also expressed (in this case Martha's desire for help). To do otherwise is usually dishonest because you are concealing necessary information from the person to whom the appeal is made.

Before looking at how Jesus responded to this and other manipulative ploys by friends and foes alike, I would like to further develop the concept of emotional manipulation.

The following chart will serve to simplify and illustrate the ways and means of childhood manipulation. The first column, Manipulative Behavior, lists some of the more common ways children tend to manipulate their parents. Remember, your child may or may not be consciously aware that he is being manipulative.

The second column, Desired Emotional Response, pinpoints what your child may be wanting his manipulative behavior to produce within you. Again remember, that your child may have practiced (gumnazo-ed) his manipulative ways so long, that at any given moment, he may not be aware of what his desires really are. Your job is to help him see what they are and that they are selfish and sinful.

The third column, Parental Reaction, identifies the foolish responses of a parent who has just been successfully manipulated by his prodigy. When this happens to you, you've just been overcome by evil rather than overcoming evil with good (Rom. 12:21).

The fourth column, Desired Controlling Effect, is the desired controlling effect that your child intends his manipulation to have on you. Your child is most likely to be aware of this one regardless of how conscious he is of the others.

The fifth column, Sinful Motives, suggests a few of the many possible motives for the manipulation. That is, it specifies those potential desires (mentioned in the last chapter) which are so intense that your child is willing to resort to manipulation (sin) in order to obtain what he wants. These motives are suggested so that you as a parent might not only better understand the source of your child's manipulation, but also help him to identify and correct the problem at its source.

Elements of Manipulative Behavior

The Behavior	Desired Emotional Response	Parental Reaction	Desired Controlling Effect	Sinful Motives
Accusations	Guilt	Defend self	To procrastinate	Love of pleasure
Criticisms	Shame	Justify actions	To avoid obligation	Love of power
Crying	Embarrassment	Blame shifting	To change parent's mind	Love of praise
"Why" questions	Hurt	Answer "why" questions	To lower parents' standard	Love of money
Obligatory Statements	Anger	Yelling back	To rescind parental punishment	Love of (anything)... food, safety, no homework, comfort, toys, freedom, a car, etc...
Sulking, Pouting				
Whining				
Withholding affection				
Cold shoulder				(see Appendix C. for additional motives)

Disrespect and Manipulation

Christ never answered a fool with a foolish response. He never fought folly with folly. In communicating with fools, He never employed communication forms that violated Scripture. Although He did respond to foolishness, He did not respond in kind. In other words, He did not allow the fool with whom He was talking to drag Him down to His level by playing the same sinful communication games as His opponent.

What He did do when responding to foolish verbiage was to show the fool his own foolishness. Those who approached Christ with the intent to manipulate Him (often by trying to make Him look foolish), walked away realizing how foolish they were themselves. The exact nature of how this was done will be discussed later in this chapter, but first you must understand the general principle of Proverbs 26:4-5. You must understand how the principle applies to your child when he is acting like the fool mentioned in Proverbs 17:21,25 who causes his parents so much pain.

A Biblical Response to Foolishness

Solomon spoke of the emotional agony associated with parenting a child who was so filled with folly that he would be classified scripturally as a "fool". *"He who begets a fool does so to his sorrow, And the father of a fool has no joy" (Prov. 17:21). "A foolish son is a grief to his father, And bitterness to her who bore him" (Prov. 17:25).* Time and space will not permit me to fully develop all of the appropriate biblical responses to a fool. There is one response, however, that must be mentioned, since out of this biblical injunction flows the essence of Christ's adeptness at dealing with manipulators. He consistently employed the wisdom of Proverbs in dealing with foolish requests, set ups, and attempts to control Him— *"Do not answer a fool according to his folly, lest you also be like him" (Prov. 26:4);* and the alternative— *"Answer a fool as his folly deserves, lest he be wise in his own eyes" (Prov. 26:4).*

The following chart contrasts the difference between answering a foolish child according to his folly and answering a foolish child as his folly deserves.

Answering A Foolish Child

According to his folly (Prov. 26:4)	As his folly deserves (Prov. 26:5)
1. You are drawn into a conflict by your child.	1. You are in control of the conversation with your child.
2. Your child is allowed to successfully employ sinful, manipuative behaviors.	2. Your child is confronted biblically when sinful, manipulative behaviors are employed.
3. You react with a snappy comeback motivated by emotions other than love for your child.	3. You respond out of love with a well thought out biblical answer that aims at driving out foolishness from the heart of your child.
4. You resort to defending yourself, justifying your actions, blame-shifting, answering "why" questions, argumentation, etc.	4. You identify and effectively put an end to your child's manipulative behavior.
5. You allow your child to terminate the conversation by having the last word before biblical correction has taken place.	5. You do not allow the conversation to end until biblical discipline and /or correction has taken place so that your child acknowledges and repents of his sin.
6. You walk away feeling guilty, intimidated, frustrated, exasperated, like a failure, and/or out of control.	6. You walk away confident that by God's grace you are in control of and successfully accomplishing the training of your child.
7. Your child walks away with the satisfaction of knowing that he has punished or manipulated you.	7. Your child walks away knowing that you have successfully thwarted his attempts at disrespect and manipulation.

Scripture records many examples of individuals who attempted to manipulate Christ. Not one person ever succeeded! In studying Christ's responses to those manipulative individuals, I have identified at least two anti-manipulation techniques that Jesus often used. These two techniques are frequently found together, but almost always at least one of them was employed.

Disrespect and Manipulation

Warning!

Before explaining what they are, I must first give a warning. Christ could not sin. His motives, therefore, for responding to the foolish requests and questions of those who wanted to manipulate Him were impeccable. He always wanted to please and glorify His father. For you to attempt to use the biblical resources that you are about to learn for selfish ends is wrong. To do so would not only be evil (the very evil you are trying to deal with biblically— manipulation), it would not be blessed by God and would likely backfire. In other words, to use biblical weapons for the purpose of fighting evil to get what you want rather than what God wants will be viewed by God as sin. It is nothing more than a gimmick to manipulate your children, not to speak of God Himself. If you expect God to bless you in your efforts to keep your children from manipulating you, you must be certain that your motives are pure before you attempt to use these resources.

Anti-Manipulation Devices

Now that you've been warned, I will explain these two anti-manipulation devices to you. They are as follows:

1. *Appeal to the personal responsibility of the manipulator* (which, typically, has not been fulfilled).

2. *Appeal to God's Word (God's Will) as the standard for judgment of the manipulator.*

For instance, let's begin by going back to the story of Mary and Martha found in Luke 10:

"Now as they were traveling along, He entered a certain village; and a woman named Martha welcomed Him into her home. And she had a sister called Mary, who moreover was listening to the Lord's word, seated at His feet. But Martha was distracted with all her preparations; and she came up to Him, and said, "Lord, do You not care that my sister has left me to do all the serving alone? Then tell her to help me." But the Lord answered and said to her, "Martha, Martha, you are worried and bothered about so many things; but only a few things are necessary, really only one, for Mary has chosen the good part, which shall not be taken away from her" (Luke 10:38-40).

The Heart of Anger

How did Christ deal with Martha's attempt to pressure Him into giving her what she wanted?

First, He made an appeal to her personal responsibilities. He said, "Martha, Martha, you are worried and bothered about so many things; but only a few things are necessary, really only one." Jesus said elsewhere that His disciples ought not to worry (Matt. 6:25) or be troubled (John 14:1). Therefore, Martha was not fulfilling at least two biblical responsibilities and Jesus reproved her. He reminded her that her only necessary responsibility was to sit at His feet and hear the Word of God.

Second, He made a subtle yet definite appeal to God's will. He said, "only a few things are necessary, really only one, for Mary has chosen the good part which shall not be taken away from her." During His own temptation when Jesus was forty days in the wilderness, He said, "Man shall not live by bread alone, but on every word that proceeds out of the mouth of God" (Matt. 4:4, Luke 4:4). Consequently, Mary, who was feasting on the Word of God, was commended for doing the good (right) thing. The fact that Jesus called what Mary had "chosen" to do "necessary" and "good" implies that she was doing God's will.

Christ's First Recorded Words

To elaborate, let's examine Christ's first recorded words. His parents were anxious when they realized that He had not returned from the Temple with them to Nazareth. When they found Him three days later *"sitting in the midst of the teachers, both listening to them and asking them questions, they were astonished", and his mother reproved Him. "Why have you treated us this way? Behold, your father and I have been anxiously looking for you" (Luke 2:48).*

Notice the use of questions. Notice the use of the "why" question, clearly used [16] to imply guilt. Notice the sympathetic appeal ("you have hurt us by making us anxious"). Perhaps you've never considered Mary's response to Jesus' behavior to be manipulative. But, whether she did so consciously or unconsciously, to the extent that she tried to make him feel guilty and or responsible for her anxiety, technically, she was using manipulation.

As you read Christ's reply, see if you can pick out the two afore-mentioned manipulation devices:

"Why is it that you were looking for me? Did you not know that I had to be in My Father's house?" (Luke 2:49)

Did you catch them?

First, Jesus appealed to personal responsibility— "Did you not know...." Mary and Joseph of all people should have known (it was their responsibility to know) that He was the Christ and that God had given Him responsibilities which He had to fulfill.

Second, Jesus made an appeal to God's will. "Did you not know that I had to be ..." Mary and Joseph should have known that Jesus had to be seeing to the affairs of His heavenly Father, not only because of the many Old Testament prophecies written about the ministry of the Messiah, but also because of what Gabriel (Luke 1:26-38), Zacharias (Luke 1:68-79), Simeon (Luke 2: 21-35), and Anna the prophetess (Luke 2: 36-38) had said concerning Him.

Against the Pharisees

Jesus used these anti-manipulation devices in another instance when He was accused of working on the Sabbath.

"Now it came about that on a certain Sabbath He was passing through some grain fields; and His disciples were picking and eating the heads of grain, rubbing them in their hands" (Luke 6:1).

On this occasion the disciples were following Christ through some fields of standing grain. As they were walking, some of the disciples began to strip off some of the grain heads into their hands. At this point, in order to remove the outer bran shell from the inner heart of each grain, they had to first rub the kernels between their hands and then blow just hard enough to scatter the light bran covering into the air and away from the heavier heart of the kernel. In the eyes of the Pharisees, who held to their traditions more tenaciously than they did to the words of Scripture, this "harvesting" was work; and consequently unlawful to perform on the Sabbath (Ex. 34:2).

"But some of the Pharisees said to Him, 'Why do you do what is not lawful on the Sabbath?'"

Did you observe once again the "why" question? In asking this question, Jesus' accusers were likely trying to discredit (embarrass) Him, or perhaps even attempting to affect His conscience with guilt. Regardless of their motive (the text does not provide it), the Pharisees were being manipulative and Christ wisely detected and responded to their manipulation.

He replied, *"Have you not even read...* (an appeal to personal responsibility: they were Pharisees and should have known the Scriptures) *what David did when he was hungry, he and those who were with him, how he entered the House of God and took and ate the consecrated bread, which is not lawful for any to eat, except the Priests alone, and gave it to his companions?"* (an appeal to God's Word: Jesus referred them to what was recorded in 1 Samuel 21:1-6 as an exception to the Law which prohibited anyone but the Priests from eating the Holy Bread of the Temple as explained in Leviticus 24:5-9). Thus, in order to press home a more important point, He compared Himself and His disciples to David and his men. In other words, Jesus said that if it was lawful for David and his men to break the law by eating the showbread, it was lawful for Him and His disciples to violate man-made traditions, because Jesus is greater than David. He is the Son of Man and the "Son of Man is Lord of the Sabbath."

Against the Chief Priests & Scribes

After telling the parable of the vineyard owner which was aimed at convicting some of the chief priests and Scribes of their rejection of Him as the Messiah, Christ became their target. Notice their clear intent to catch Him.

"And the scribes and the chief priests tried to lay hands on Him that very hour, and they feared the people; for they understood that He spoke this parable against them. And they watched Him, and sent

spies who pretended to be righteous, in order that they might catch Him in some statement, so as to deliver Him up to the rule and the authority of the governor. And they questioned Him, saying, 'Teacher, we know that You speak and teach correctly, and You are not partial to any, but teach the way of God in truth. Is it lawful for us to pay taxes to Caesar, or not?'"(Luke 20:19-22)

Notice also their flattery (verse 21), which was no doubt intended to make them look sincere in front of the people. Again, they use a question (verse 22) and limit His choices to only two options, yes or no. They set Him up to be disreputable in the eyes of either the people or the government. As you consider the remainder of the text, notice His detection of their manipulation (verse 23), His answering a question with a question (verse 24), the employment of His two favorite anti-manipulation weapons (verse 25), and the silencing effect they had on His manipulators (verse 26).

"But He detected their trickery and said to them, 'Show Me a denarius. Whose likeness and inscription does it have?' And they said, 'Caesar's.' And He said to them, 'Then render to Caesar the things that are Caesar's, and to God the things that are God's.' And they were unable to catch Him in a saying in the presence of the people; and marveling at His answer, they became silent" (Luke 20:23-26).

Could you pick out the two devices? They were:

1. *Appeal to Personal Responsibility*— (A direct command: "Then render to Caesar...") It was their responsibility to obey Caesar and pay taxes as it was their responsibility to honor God with the first portion of their increase.

2. *Appeal to God's Will*— They were to give God that which the Scripture says rightfully belonged to Him. "...and (render) to God the things that are God's." The word "render" means "to give or do something necessary in fulfillment of an obligation or expectation." [17]

Time and space prohibit me from illustrating our Lord's employment of these two means of "answering a fool as his folly deserves" any further in this chapter. To reduce the wealth of insight that can be gained by studying all of Christ's responses in these situations would be to diminish His infinite wisdom, and to miss many additional important truths other than the two on which this chapter has focused. Yet, I believe these two principles are vitally important in learning how to respond to manipulative people in general, and manipulative children in particular. The next chapter is devoted to the application of these two principles in training children, especially those children who struggle with anger.

How to Conquer Disrespect and Manipulation

The development of the material in this chapter began years ago as I was attempting to teach a young mother how to deal with her disrespectful son. I asked her to keep a journal to record a "blow by blow" verbatim account of the dialogue with her son during times of conflict. During each session, I unpacked the journal, diagnosing each wrong verbal exchange biblically. Then, I helped her repack the conflict biblically. Our goal was for the son to learn how to communicate his desires without being disrespectful. The mother was to learn how to detect and conquer manipulative behavior in her son. I found this method to be beneficial, and thus developed the Conflict Journal. (See Appendix E. beginning on page 187 for a sample you can photocopy for your use.)

The Conflict Journal

In the following example of the Conflict Journal, notice how the teen cleverly distracted her mother by manipulation. Notice also how the mother responded in kind and answered a fool according to ("in the same way as") her folly.

The Heart of Anger

CONFLICT JOURNAL (sample)

Circumstances surrounding the conflict:

After coming home from school Phyllis was asked by her mother to clean up her room.

Mom: "Go upstairs and clean your room."
Phyllis: "But, it's not dirty."

Mom: "Yes it is!"
Phyllis: "You're always asking me to clean my room."

Mom: "I am not!"
Phyllis: "You don't keep your room as clean as you expect me to keep mine. You didn't even make your bed this morning!"

Mom: "You don't have half the responsibilities that I do."
Phyllis: "None of my friends have to clean their rooms everyday."

Mom: "That may be true, but you have to live with us not with them."
Phyllis: "Why is it so important to you that I clean my room every day?"

Mom: "Because it is a house rule, I'm your mother, and I told you to."
Phyllis: "Oh, all right. I'll do it after supper."

Mom: "You'll do it now!"
Phyllis: "But Mom, Johnny and I are going to the mall. He'll be here any minute."

Mom: "You're not going anywhere until your room is clean young lady!"
Phyllis: "You don't love me! You don't understand me! All you care about is your precious little house. I can't wait until I can leave home. (Phyllis storms up to her room, crying and stomping her feet, murmuring under her breath, and slamming the bedroom door.)

At this point Phyllis' mother is likely feeling guilty, out of control, confused, angry (frustrated), ashamed or incapable of being an effective parent. Her daughter has successfully outsmarted her through manipulation. Phyllis has also managed to successfully procrastinate.

For the sake of simplicity, and since dealing with disrespect has been covered in a previous chapter, I will only unpack and repack the mother's responses to her daughter's manipulation. I will, however, identify the manipulative behavior on the daughter's part. Please keep in mind that the alternative responses I suggest are only representative of dozens— perhaps thousands— of equally effective biblical responses. Be especially alert to the use of the two aforementioned anti-manipulation techniques.

For illustrative purposes, I have borrowed a concept from the world of boxing, which is a biblical concept (cf. 1 Cor. 9:26; Eph. 6:2; Col. 1:29; Heb. 12:4), breaking down the entire conflict into individual "rounds."

Round One:

Mother: "Go upstairs and clean your room."
Phyllis: "But it is not dirty."

Here Phyllis is calling into question her mother's presupposition that Phyllis' room is dirty. In other words, she is saying, "It is wrong for you to ask me to clean my room because your request is not based on accurate information."

Mother: "Yes it is!"

At this point, Phyllis' mother begins to answer a fool according to her folly. She allows herself to be lured into a verbal snare designed to disarm her of her parental authority. If Phyllis does trick Mom into fighting in her own corner rather than in the one in with which her mom is more familiar, then Phyllis will gain the advantage. Mom should not let this happen. If Mom's data is inaccurate there is an appeal process (discussed in Chapter Twelve) that may be employed by Phyllis to make her point without being manipulative (i.e. "Mother, I understand that you want me to clean my room and I am certainly willing to do that. I do, however, have some new information that I would like you to consider. May I present that information to you?").

Appropriate Biblical Response: "Sweetheart, if you are trying to make an appeal, that is not how it is done. I have seen your room, and it simply is not acceptable. Your responsibility according to Scripture is to obey your parents, and I expect you to obey me. If, after you clean your room, you would like to discuss our family standards of cleanliness, I will be happy to do so provided you discuss them without being disrespectful."

Round Two:

Phyllis: "You always ask me to clean my room."

Here we most likely have a subtle manipulative appeal for reasonableness or justice. Perhaps Phyllis is trying to say, "Mom, you are a fanatic about my room. You're a slave driver. Why don't you lighten up and stop being such a tyrant? You're not being reasonable and I don't think that's very fair." Phyllis may be trying to evoke guilt or perhaps sympathy in her mother to get her to back off.

Mother: "I am not!"

Again mother allows herself to be lured into Phyllis' snare. She is lured away from the corner given her by God into the corner of her beloved opponent/adversary. She has once again answered a fool according to her folly, and her daughter still remains wise in her own eyes.

Appropriate Biblical Response: Assuming that Mom lost round one by answering a fool according to her folly rather than by answering a fool as her folly deserves, she still may recover in round two. Don't forget, if you, as a parent, should lose the first few rounds because you didn't detect the manipulation soon enough, you have not lost the fight. At any point in the necessary battle, you may recover and deliver the knock-out blow *("Do not be overcome with evil but overcome evil with good" Rom. 12:21.)*, by using the state-of-the-art weaponry with which God has provided and wielding it effectively.

Mom should have said, "God asks you always to honor your parents and to obey them unless they ask you to sin. It is not a sin for you to clean your room. It is a sin (for which there will be consequences) to dishonor and disobey your mother as you are doing right now."

Round Three:

Phyllis: "You don't keep your room as clean as you expect me to keep mine. You didn't even make your bed this morning."

Phyllis is now bringing out the heavy artillery. She has switched from throwing a few left jabs to heaving a right hook at her mother's conscience. If she can inflict a wound severe enough to produce guilt she will win this round— perhaps even the whole fight.

Phyllis:"You hypocrite!" "How dare you ask me to do one thing and you practice another. Why, you are provoking me to anger with your double standards. I've read that Angry Kids book too, you know."

Mom: "You don't have half the responsibilities that I do!"

Oops! She did it again. She took the bait. She fell for it once more. She has allowed herself to be diverted away from the real issue (her daughter's sin) by the clever smoke screen of guilt. She is answering a foolish accusation rather than rebuking it.

Appropriate Biblical Response: Assuming again, for the sake of illustration, that Mom lost the first two rounds, here is one way she may rebound in the third.

"Honey, right now your heart needs cleaning more than both of our rooms. You may go to the Think Room until you are able to continue this conversation according to biblical principles. If you persist in your manipulation, you will leave me no choice but to discipline you for your sinful attitude. The punishment will be to clean my room and your room for one week. You need to make the decision, Dear."

The Heart of Anger

Round Four:

Phyllis: "None of my friends have to clean their rooms every day."

Having scored a few points with the right hook, Phyllis now abruptly changes to a left upper-cut, hoping to catch her mother off guard. By comparing her "unreasonable" mother to the "reasonable" mothers of her companions, she once again hopes to stun her opponent with another blow to the conscience: "Only a tyrannical slave-driving bully would require her child to clean her room every day," she implies. "Compared to any standard of rationality, no parent ought to require her child to clean her room every day!"

Mom: "That may be true, but you have to live with us and not with them."

Appropriate biblical response: You might say "That sounds like a good response to me." Perhaps it is better than the previous responses but it still does not pinpoint personal culpability. In other words, Phyllis' Mom may have deflected the upper-cut a little but Phyllis still gets a point or two for connecting. An even better response, would be, "You are not only being manipulative, you are being unwise. The Bible says *'When they measure themselves by themselves and compare themselves with themselves, they are without understanding' (2 Cor. 10:12)*. You are procrastinating and being disobedient and now I must discipline you."

"But I never would have thought of that Scripture. I don't know the Bible that well," you say. But Jesus did, and because He did, no one ever successfully manipulated Him. The simple truth is, the more of God's Word you have internalized, the better equipped you are to deal with manipulation. When you are stumped about what to say (i.e. when you lose a round), remember what your child said to deliver the unchallenged blow. Then go to your Bible, research an appropriate answer including Scripture *("The heart of the righteous ponders how to answer." Prov. 15:28)*, so that next time you will be prepared to defend against the blow and counter it with biblical wisdom.

Round Five:

Phyllis: "Why is it so important to you that I clean my room?"

When all else fails, duck and counter with the left jab "why." "Why" is probably the best way for a manipulator to catch an opponent off guard, forcing him to defend himself and making him more vulnerable to an immediate, more punishing blow. "Why," you remember, was the favorite manipulative tool of the religious leaders who tried to set up Jesus. "You seem to have a need for my room to be clean" is the innuendo. "Could it be that you are a compulsive, perfectionistic 'cleannick' who is in need of 'professional help?'" This jab is aimed at Mom's pride. It is an attack on her character.

Mom: "Because it's a house rule and I told you to."

Phyllis' mother defends herself against the attack, but does so in such a way as to give credibility to the question. Additionally, rather than appeal to the Scripture, Mom appeals to a lower standard that is easily attacked. ("Well then, the house rules are too strict." or "Mother, you're always telling me to do the things you want me to.") Mom should have responded without giving credibility to Phyllis' question. Instead, she should have appealed to the authority of Scripture which may never rightly be challenged.

Appropriate Biblical Response: "Sweetheart, you ought to be more concerned about what's important to the Lord like obeying your parents. If you cannot persuade your father and me to change our minds after one respectful appeal you must assume that it is the Lord's will for you to clean your room to our specifications."

Round Six:

Phyllis: "Oh, all right, I'll do it after supper."

Phyllis intellectually realized that she is not going to change her mother's mind, unreasonable as it may be. She grudgingly concedes to obey, but she is going to determine when to obey. It's hard to deny that her mother finally connected for some points.

The Heart of Anger

Phyllis is not going to admit that it hurt. So she steps back out of range, throws her arms up in the air, and shrugs her shoulders as if to say, "That didn't hurt." Then she tries to clinch her mother's arms with procrastination (a promise of delayed obedience).

Mom: "You'll do it now."

It looks like Mom is starting to rally, but remember this is the sixth round. More importantly, although Mom is getting stronger, her punches still lack the authority of Scripture. It is now a matter of Mom's will verses the daughter's will. It should be made a matter of God's will versus the daughter's will.

Appropriate Biblical Response: Assuming once again that Mother has allowed the conflict to go on to this point undetected or uncontrolled she may respond as follows.

"Delayed obedience is disobedience. Please do not assume that you'll be eating supper in this house until you've cleaned up your room and repented of your disobedience as God requires."

Round Seven:

Phyllis: "But, Mom, Johnny and I are going to the shopping mall. He'll be here any minute."

"That's illegal" she protests "you're stepping on my foot and hitting me with the back of your elbow. I can't believe you're going to make me clean my room when I've made previous plans. You're denying my personhood. You're imposing your will on mine, and I don't think that's fair! Foul! Foul!" All of this amounts to a left jab straight to the conscience.

Mom: "You're not going anywhere until your room is clean."

Again, Mom is getting stronger, trying to enforce her God given parental authority. Yet, by adding something else, Mom's answer can be even stronger.

Appropriate Biblical Response: "You are not going anywhere until you first obey me as the Lord expects you to by cleaning your room. Then, we will disassemble and reconstruct biblically the disrespectful and manipulative communication you've chosen to bring to our conflict. And finally, you will not go to the mall until I am convinced that you are truly repentant in your heart."

In addition to strengthening the appeal to personal responsibly, Mom added a reference to God's will. Here Mom has required Phyllis to exercise herself for the purpose of godliness, including biblical examination of her thoughts and motives.

Round Eight:

Phyllis realizes that Mom is beginning to score more and more points. If this keeps up her Mom may win the fight. This requires drastic measures. It's time to go for the knock out. In a battery of guilt producing punches, most of which are illegal because they are below the belt, Phyllis hurls all of her energy into a weighty emotional knockout attempt.

Phyllis: "You don't love me, you don't understand me. All you care about is your precious little house. I can't wait until I can leave home!"

After that she storms up to her room, crying, stomping her feet, murmuring under her breath, and slamming the bedroom door behind her.

Phyllis has just scored a TKO (Technical Knock Out). She has succeeded in provoking her mother into feeling so guilty, angry, ashamed, incompetent and confused that she throws in the towel. Phyllis has just won her twelfth bout of manipulation against her mother this month.

Did you catch the two anti-manipulation techniques in each of the appropriate biblical responses? If not, reread each response until you can identify both appeals. Let me emphasize again that the responses given in this dialogue are only examples of many possible biblically correct responses, each of which may vary greatly depending on circumstances, personality, and overall character of both parent and child.

Biblical Guidelines For Responding to Childhood Manipulation

At this point I must insert another warning! Previously I warned you of the dangers involved in using these procedures with wrong motives. Now I must tell you that if your methods of using these resources do not follow other biblical guidelines, you may not expect God to honor your efforts. In other words, if you desire to glorify God by using these procedures, you must do so in accordance with other God-honoring biblical procedures. You must do the right thing in the right way.

More importantly, as with all of the resources in this book, you must truly be a Christian and have the Spirit of God residing inside of you to enable and empower you to use these tools. If you have not acknowledged your sin and put your trust in Christ's substitutionary death on the cross, you simply will not be able to consistently apply the instruction you've received in this book. Christ Jesus substituted Himself in place of sinners that those who "believe in Him might not perish but have eternal life." Only those who through faith accept what He has done by taking on Himself the punishment which they deserve, receive eternal life and the Holy Spirit, who provides the power to obey the Bible. Without the indwelling Spirit of God in your life, there is no possibility that you will be able to obey God's command to "not provoke your children to anger; but bring them up in the discipline and instruction of the Lord." With the Spirit of God residing in your life, you will be able to increasingly and effectively apply all of the God-given resources explained in the book.

Here then are five guidelines that will help you to do the right thing (conquer manipulation and disrespect in your child) in the right way:

Examine your motives: Your motives for responding to your child's manipulation should be righteous. The goal of your instruction should be love (1 Tim. 1:5). You should not desire to belittle or embarrass him, nor censure or criticize him, nor show off your own cleverness or verbal prowess in front of him. You should never respond to manipulative behavior from a motive of personal retaliation or vengeance.

Examine your life: According to Galatians 6:1, as you attempt to restore your sinning brother you should be "looking to yourself, lest you too be tempted." In other words, you should examine your own life for any sinful words, actions, and attitudes (especially manifestations of the same basic tendencies of disrespect and manipulation). Remember, "hypocrite" was the word Jesus used to describe those who do not examine and remove the log from their own eye before speaking to others about the speck in theirs (Matt. 7:3-5).

Maintain a spirit of gentleness: When your child sins against God, it may evoke in you righteous anger (or indignation). If, however, you are more angry that your child is sinning against you than you are because his sin is against God, what you are likely experiencing is sinful anger. Restoring your brother (child) "in a spirit of gentleness" (or meekness; Gal. 6:1) means that you do so without being sinfully angry yourself. You see, it is possible for righteous anger and sinful anger to reside in your heart at the same time. Before you open your mouth to reprove your manipulating child, you had better be sure that any anger you may feel in your heart is due to his sin *against God* rather than his sin *against you*. And, if you are certain that you can speak out of such a righteous anger, you had better take heed that such anger does not express itself in sinful forms of communication. Angry forms of communication include such things as:

Harshness

"A gentle answer turns away wrath, but a harsh word stirs up anger" (Prov. 15:1).

Biting Sarcasm

"And they stripped Him, and put a scarlet robe on Him. And after weaving a crown of thorns, they put it on His head, and a reed in His right hand; and they kneeled down before

The Heart of Anger

Him and mocked Him, saying, 'Hail, King of the Jews!'"
(Matt. 27:28-29)

Raising Your Voice

"A gentle answer turns away wrath, but a harsh word stirs up anger" (Prov 15:1).

Profanity

"Let no unwholesome word proceed from your mouth, but only such (a word) as is good for edification according to the need (of the moment,) that it may give grace to those who hear" (Eph. 4:29).

Name Calling

"And Paul, looking intently at the Council, said, 'Brethren, I have lived my life with a perfectly good conscience before God up to this day.' And the high priest Ananias commanded those standing beside him to strike him on the mouth. Then Paul said to him, 'God is going to strike you, you whitewashed wall! And do you sit to try me according to the Law, and in violation of the Law order me to be struck?' But the bystanders said, 'Do you revile God's high priest?' And Paul said, 'I was not aware, brethren, that he was high priest; for it is written, "You shall not speak evil of a ruler of your people"'" (Acts 23:1-5).

Throwing, Kicking or Hitting Things

"An overseer, then, must be above reproach, the husband of one wife, temperate, prudent, respectable, hospitable, able to teach, not addicted to wine or pugnacious, but gentle, uncontentious, free from the love of money" (1 Tim 3:2-3).

False Accusations

"You shall not bear false witness against your neighbor" (Exod. 20:16).

Criticism (having a judgmental or critical spirit)

"Do not speak against one another, brethren. He who speaks against a brother, or judges his brother, speaks against

the law, and judges the law; but if you judge the law, you are not a doer of the law, but a judge (of it). There is (only) one Lawgiver and Judge, the One who is able to save and to destroy; but who are you who judge your neighbor?"
(James 4:11-12)

Pouting or Sulking

"But Jezebel his wife came to him and said to him, "How is it that your spirit is so sullen that you are not eating food?" So he said to her, "Because I spoke to Naboth the Jezreelite, and said to him, 'Give me your vineyard for money; or else, if it pleases you, I will give you a vineyard in its place.' But he said, 'I will not give you my vineyard'"
(1 Kings 21:5, 6).

Choose the right words: You must speak the truth in love. You must select words that communicate grace and that will meet the needs of your child, for the purpose of edifying him. *"Let no unwholesome word proceed from your mouth, but only such (a word) as is good for edification according to the need (of the moment,) that it may give grace to those who hear" (Eph. 4:29).* As a parent, you must *"let your speech always be with grace, seasoned, (as it were,) with salt, so that you may know how you should respond to each person" (Col. 4:6) (my words added in parenthesis for understanding).*

Remember that these anti-manipulation devices are only one small part of your biblical parenting resources: There are many biblical tools with which you have been provided to train your children in Christlike character. Doctrine, reproof, correction, and disciplined training in righteousness are the essential elements. *"All Scripture is inspired by God and profitable for teaching, for reproof, for correction, for training in righteousness . . ." (2 Tim 3:16).* All other biblically legitimate means and methods of parenting fall under these four. Corporal punishment (spanking), biblical communication principles, The Gumnazo Principle, the various journals explained in this book, and any other valid biblical methodology found in any other book is valid only to the extent that it is used in a way that is consistent with and subordinate to this four fold process of change. The anti-manipulation technique outlined in this book is no exception. It must be used as a part of the system, in the entire milieu of biblical parenting.

To allow this (or any other) concept to become the predominant modus operandi of your parenting, is to distort the application of biblical truth and present a biblically unbalanced view of Christianity to your child. It is to rip out that small slice of the pie, magnify it several times larger than its actual size and superimpose it over the rest of the pie (making it the predominant piece). It will provoke your children to anger rather than bring them up in the discipline and instruction of the Lord. So, be careful that you balance this powerful biblical resource with all the rest.

Sharpening Your Skills

If you desire to become proficient in your ability to deal effectively with your child's manipulation, you will have to practice (gumnazo) implementing what you've just learned. You must become at least as good at preventing manipulation as your child is at attempting it. My counselees occasionally express incredulity at my ability to quickly and biblically answer some of the questions that have stumped them for months or even years. What they often fail to realize is that for months and even years, I've sat in the same chair, stumped by those same questions asked me by numerous other counselees. It was only after being stumped and then searching Scripture for the right answer that I have, by God's grace, become increasingly adept at answering tough questions. It is only as you, Christian parent, go back to the Scripture and study how to respond to the foolish and verbal maneuverings of your little schemer, that you will become increasingly more adept at answering his manipulative rhetoric.

The Manipulation Worksheet

I developed the manipulation worksheet to help counselees study how to answer manipulative individuals and to train themselves (gumnazo) how to "answer a fool as his folly deserves" (see Appendix E. for a sample to photocopy and use). Once you begin recognizing your child's manipulative ploys, (in other words, you lose a round because you didn't have a wise answer) take out the worksheet and commence pondering. The following is an explanation of the four sections and how to best use them:

1. Circumstances Surrounding Manipulation

Recording the circumstances which surround the manipulation will insure that the transgression is examined in its proper context. You will be better able to detect common denominators or patterns of what triggers the manipulation and the times at which the manipulation occurs.

2. Manipulative Remarks Made To Me

Recording verbatim (or as accurately as possible) the words chosen by the tactician will help you break down cunning subterfuge into its component parts. As you examine each manipulative remark, try to detect the following:

▸ *The exact form of manipulative behavior (accusations, "why" questions, obligatory statements, etc.)*

▸ *The possible desired emotional response (guilt, shame, fear, etc.)*

▸ *The possible desired controlling effect (procrastination, lowering of standards, etc.)*

▸ *The possible sinful motives (love of pleasure, power, praise, etc.)*

At this point, I must raise two notes of warning. First, you may judge actions and words, but you may not judge thoughts and motives without confirmation. The reason for examining "possible" internal areas are for use later on in helping the child examine his own heart (i.e. "Could it be that the reason you said that was to make me feel guilty?"). When your child examines his own heart and confirms verbally that his thoughts and motives are wrong, you may (if necessary) reprove him for attitude sins.

Second, you must be sure that the remarks which you perceived as manipulative, truly were manipulative (i.e. you had better be certain that you have enough evidence to make the manipulation diagnosis). To do otherwise would be to answer a matter before hearing it and to have it be folly and shame to you (Prov. 18:13).

Some individuals are given to inaccurate perceptions and tend to perceive inoffensive words as if given with malicious intent. Others who are proud (hypersensitive is the more fashionable but less biblical word today) tend to overreact in a similar fashion. When they detect the lightest disesteem, rebuke or criticism, regardless of how valid, they are prone to perceive such things as an attack against them. If you are personally given to such misperceptions, you might consider enlisting the help of another believer (perhaps a spouse) whose judgment is better than yours in such matters to help you diagnose manipulative behavior more accurately.

3. My Response to the Manipulation

My purpose in asking you to fill in this worksheet is to examine a conflict as though you were looking at a video tape of a boxing match after losing the fight. You've just watched it observing the style, technique and strategy of your opponent so that you can learn how to prevail against him in the future. Now you're going to rewind the tape and view it a second time, looking for your mistakes to plan ahead for the next confrontation. This is yet another part of the training (gumnazo) process.

Having confirmed that you have indeed been manipulated, you are now going to record verbatim (or as accurately as possible) how you responded to the manipulator. As you consider your answer, notice how your opponent got you off track by focusing on something other than his responsibility and notice the bait he used to lure you into his snare. Work at identifying your emotions, thoughts, and motives and evaluate them biblically (you should remember how to do this from the previous chapter). Pinpoint your exact "parental reaction" (defending self, answering "why" questions, blame-shifting, etc.). Understanding your vulnerability in these areas will prepare you for future manipulative attempts.

4. Christlike (Biblical) Response to the Manipulation

This is the most important part of the worksheet; it is at this point that you reconstruct your answer to reflect the wisdom of Christ. Here is where you determine how to integrate into your response one or both of the scriptural anti-manipulation techniques discussed in this chapter. You must consider your child's level of maturity, his consciousness of his manipulative ways, the degree of firmness that is to be used, the consequences (if any) that are to be brought to bear on him should he continue not to respond biblically, and any other extenuating or unusual circumstances that pertain to the issue at hand. This will take time, but it will be time well invested as your levels of skill and confidence will increase in direct proportion to your investment.

Study the following sample worksheet. After reading each parental response, but *before* you read the Christlike (biblical) response, practice constructing your own biblical response.

MANIPULATION WORKSHEET (*sample*)

Circumstances surrounding manipulation:
At 9:15 Saturday morning Tommy was visited by some friends who invited him to play baseball with them. When he asked my permission, I explained that he would not be able to play ball due to a check-up appointment that we both had at the dentist that morning.

1. Manipulative remarks made to me:
"But Mom, my teeth are fine! I didn't have any cavities last time. You go to the dentist by yourself, and I'll stay home and play ball."

2. My response to the manipulation:
"I don't think that's a good idea honey, you'd better come with me."

3. Christlike (biblical) response to the manipulation: [19]
"Honey, that is not the way to make an appeal. You're not to give me directions. The Bible says that you are to follow my directions. Would you please try that again in a more respectful manner?"

The Heart of Anger

1. Manipulative remarks made to me:

"But, why?"

2. My response to the manipulation:

"Because we have an appointment."

3. Christlike (biblical) response to the manipulation:

"Son, you are being manipulative and disobedient and that is wrong. If, after we go to the dentist, you haven't figured out the answer to that question, I'll be happy to explain the answer to you provided you can ask it the right way."

1. Manipulative remarks made to me:

"But, I never get to play ball with these guys."

2. My response to the manipulation:

"Oh, yes you do! You played with them just two weeks ago. Don't you remember?"

3. Christlike (biblical) response to the manipulation:

"Are you more interested in playing ball or in pleasing the Lord?"

1. Manipulative remarks made to me:

"Why do you always schedule the things that I hate to do on the weekends? You should make these doctors appointments on school days so that I could have fun on the weekends."

2. My response to the manipulation:

"But, Dear, you know that's not always possible. Besides, I have other responsibilities which I must attend to during the week, and, therefore, I cannot always take you places then."

3. Christlike (biblical) response to the manipulation:

"You should desire to please the Lord by honoring and obeying your parents more than you desire to have fun on the weekends as well as during the week. To the extent that you do not, you are a 'lover of pleasure' rather than a 'lover of God'" (cf. 2 Tim. 3:4).

1. Manipulative remark made to me:

"You're just too busy. You need to stay home more and take better care of me."

2. My response to the manipulation:

"I am not too busy! And what's wrong with the way I take care of you?"

3. Christlike (biblical) response to the manipulation:

"Honey, the real problem is that you are too willful. I think you need to be grounded from playing ball of any kind until you examine your words, attitudes, thoughts, actions, and motives in light of God's word, and until you can convince me that you have changed them all."

1. Manipulative remarks made to me:

"I never have any fun with my friends. I have social needs too, you know. You need to let me have more time with my friends so that I can develop socially."

2. My response to the manipulation:

"What kind of social needs? Where did you learn that term?"

3. Christlike (biblical) response to the manipulation:

"You have more spiritual needs right now than you have social ones, Dear. What you need more than time with your friends is time with the Lord developing the character that will best enable you to develop socially.

Besides, right now your parents are your closest neighbors and God's second greatest command is to 'love your neighbor as (with the same intensity that) you love yourself' (Matt. 22:39). Sweetheart, you have been violating this command since this conversation began."

1. Manipulative remarks made to me:

"Forget it! You don't really care and you wouldn't change even if you did. Let's go to the dentist." (At which point Tommy droops his head, slouches his shoulder and schleps off to his room, sulking, pouting, and giving me the cold shoulder.)

2. My response to the manipulation:

(Nothing! I can't believe he did it to me again!)

3. Christlike (biblical) response to the manipulation:

"Please come back here young man! This conversation is far from over. You don't seem to care about pleasing God today. After I discipline you, you may go to the Think Room. Perhaps there you will be able, with the Lord's help, to readjust your affections. When you are ready to confess and repent of your bad attitudes, you may come out and together we will go to God's Word to diagnose and correct your sinful attitude. And Honey, if we have not finished doing so by the time we get back from the dentist, we will continue addressing these issues after we return."

How did you do? I hope you did well. Remember there are many possible wise answers. You may even prefer your own responses to the ones I've recorded.

If you did not detect at least one of the two anti-manipulation techniques in every Christlike/biblical response then you have missed something. If so, perhaps you should reread the first section of this chapter again to reacquaint yourself with the two concepts. Your most important mission is to practice with this worksheet (or a similar one of your own making) any and every time you walk away from a conflict where you feel like a fool. When this occurs the chances are you answered a fool "according to his folly" rather than answering him "as his folly deserves."

The Think Room

At various places throughout this book I have mentioned The Think Room and I have promised to provide additional information about it. You have patiently waited (I know that some of you, who believe that you must process your data sequentially, have searched through the book prematurely and read this portion), and now it is time to keep that promise.

First, however, I must give another warning. One of the greatest fears a teacher has is that someone will take his words and distort them in a way that dishonors God by misuse or misapplication of the truth he presented. As a counselor, I have, more often than I can count, had counselees twist and distort truth into something that was patently unbiblical while they were explaining a concept to someone else (usually a pastor). I've heard of at least one teacher who was subpoenaed to court to explain his biblical views on corporal punishment because one of his students, who was being accused of child abuse, implicated him as the one who had taught him to spank his children.

What It's Not

With this in mind, I am going to begin by explaining up front what The Think Room is not. The primary intent of The Think Room is *not* punishment. That is, it is not meant to be a form of chastisement such as spanking and should not be used as a substitute for it. It is not another name for "Time Out". Neither is the primary purpose of The Think Room isolation from others. Isolation typically involves removal of benefits of social interaction as a form of punishment for wrong doing. The primary intent of The Think Room is education, that the child may "study" how to respond ("answer" Prov. 15:28) biblically rather than sinfully to his parents. The temporary loss of social interaction is a by-product of spending time rethinking an issue biblically. For most children, to critically evaluate their thinking biblically while interacting with others would be counter-productive (if not impossible).

Neither is The Think Room to be used vindictively. As a parent you must never execute personal retribution (vengeance) on your child. Such action would not only be a clear violation of "never take your own revenge" (Rom. 12:19) but, as mentioned earlier, would likely provoke your child to anger (Eph. 6:4).

The purpose of The Think Room is instruction, not destruction. The Think Room is a place that is conducive to meditation and reflection. It is not a dungeon in which to lock up children who do not obey or honor their parents. It is a place that should be used to improve the parent child relationship, not a place for abusing it.

What It Is

What then is The Think Room? The Think Room is a place in your home that has been designated for a child to go while he is "studying how to answer" his parents in a biblical manner.

"The heart of the righteous studies how to answer . . ." (*Prov. 15:28* NKJV). It is a temporary, open-ended form of discipline that is more corrective than retributive in nature. It is temporary and open-ended in that after a ten to fifteen minute period, your child is allowed to return to the family to correct his behavior. He remains in The Think Room only as long as it takes him to determine an appropriate biblical response to you.

What To Do While in The Think Room

Concepts to be studied by the child while in the Think Room include such things as:

The Think Room

▶ *A biblical diagnosis of previous sinful behavior (words, actions, attitudes, and motives),*

▶ *Alternative biblical replacements for such sinful behavior,*

▶ *The exact wording for asking forgiveness of sinful behavior,*

▶ *An alternative biblical response (words, tone of voice, nonverbal communication) to specific parental instruction, reproof, correction, questions, and training (see Appendix B.),*

▶ *The completion of the various journals mentioned in this book (Anger Journal, Heart Journal, etc.),*

▶ *Any other topic that your child must biblically rethink.*

When To Use The Think Room

Since the purpose of The Think Room is to study, the atmosphere of The Think Room should be conducive to learning. It should be a place where there are no pleasures (television, music, play things, etc.) or distractions from other people. For most children, this would exclude their own bedroom. The Think Room environment should also include good lighting, a table, a Bible, a concordance, other books (dictionary, thesaurus, biblical cross references, etc.), a list of the six items listed above, and something on which to record data all of which should be accessible to the child. The Think Room is best situated in a part of the house where your child will, on one hand, be comfortable enough to study, yet, on the other hand, not be so comfortable that he would desire to stay there indefinitely. Ideally, a guest room, study or den works well, as does a dining room or possibly a kitchen (provided distractions from adjacent rooms are not too great). The exact location is not nearly as important as are the environmental conditions.

The Think Room and Younger Children

For a younger child this technique works quite well when modified somewhat. For example, a three year old may be told to go to her room to think about the way she is acting and to pray. She may be told to come out of her room when she can come out with a happy attitude (and ask forgiveness if necessary).

When my daughter Sophia had just turned two, she surprised us by implementing this practice almost on her own. My wife, Kim, had given her some instructions about which she was attempting to begin a temper tantrum. Kim quickly picked her up, put her on her bed, and told her she was to lie on her bed until she could quit crying and have a good attitude. (If she had not changed her attitude soon, she would have been disciplined.) My wife then left the room to continue some chores. Only a couple of minutes later, our little daughter, who has always been very verbal for her age, came to my wife and said, "Mommy, I feel better now, I prayed to Jesus." Kim was quite pleasantly surprised, she had not thought to ask her to pray, but Sophia had taken the initiative to do so. Kim asked her what she had prayed to Jesus about. Sophia replied, "I ask Jesus to help me lie down and not be selfish." Children are sometimes capable of understanding and doing more than we give them credit for.

The Think Room and Older Children

With an older child, when the parent deems it necessary to use The Think Room he should instruct his child to go there, giving him precise instructions on the following:

1. The minimum amount of time to be spent there (usually 5-15 minutes)— "you are to go to The Think Room for at least 10 minutes." This tends to keep a child from coming up with a hastily devised or flippant answer.

2. The exact nature or purpose of the training exercise. "You are being disrespectful. You are to go to The Think Room for at least 10 minutes to figure out a more respectful way to respond to me."

3. The specific assignment (project) that is to be completed before returning from The Think room. "Before you come back to our discussion you should be prepared to ask my forgiveness for being disrespectful and demonstrate at least

two biblically better ways to respectfully make the point you just tried to make disrespectfully.

As mentioned earlier, The Think Room may be used before, during or after chastisement. Before chastisement The Think Room may be used as a preventive measure to defuse a potential behavioral time bomb. "You are developing a sarcastic attitude. You'd better spend five minutes in The Think Room and do an Anger Journal before you do something for which I must discipline you."

After your child has sinned, as an integral part of the disciplinary process (while the chastisement is in effect), The Think Room may be utilized. "You have disobeyed me again. This offense cannot be overlooked. You have left me no choice but to suspend telephone privileges for one week. Additionally, I want you to spend at least fifteen minutes in The Think Room working on a Heart Journal so that you can figure out just what it was that you wanted so much that you were willing to sin in order to have it. Then, together we will figure out from Scripture what can be done to dethrone that idol in your heart."

In some cases the chastisement is more effectively administered first. Then, when your child's attention has been secured, The Think Room can be utilized to help prepare him for further instruction.

For example: "I have tolerated your disrespect as long as I can, but that last remark is biblically intolerable. You will be spanked for dishonoring your mother, my wife, that way." Then, after administering corporal punishment in a manner consistent with Scripture and without provoking the child to further anger, you should say, "Before we reassemble and review the last few verbal exchanges between you and your mother, I want you to spend some time in The Think Room (at least 10 minutes) confessing the dishonoring of your mother to the Lord, preparing to ask her forgiveness, and thinking through some biblical responses to her." [20]

On occasion, more than one trip to The Think Room may be in order. This is done when your child continues to show an uncooperative or unrepentant spirit. As a rule, however, as long as he maintains a teachable spirit, you should help "fine tune" his responses without sending him back to the designated area.

Remember, The Think Room does not complete the training (gumnazo) process; but rather conditions your child for it. Completion of the process occurs after your child has returned from their time in The Think Room, and has accomplished two things. First, he has reviewed and diagnosed his sinful behavior. Second, he has rethought and restructured it into biblically acceptable behavior in your presence and with your assistance as his parent, if necessary. Remember that behavior encompasses not just words, attitudes and actions, but his thoughts and motives as well. Remember also that you have not completed the training process until your child has both reviewed and rethought his sinful behavior and has rehearsed these issues properly to your satisfaction.

The Appeal Process

Another tool I have mentioned previously is the appeal. [21] The process of making an appeal is one of several biblical resources whereby a child (or anyone in a position of subordination) may protect himself from abusive or tyrannical authorities. It is a balance to the principle of submission to authority taught in the Bible. Time and space will not permit development of the other resources and balances in this book. But the appeal has been included because it is especially effective in dealing with angry children.

The Scriptures contain a good number of appeals made by various individuals in different ways for many reasons. Various words are used in Scripture to convey the concept of an appeal. Nehemiah appealed to King Artaxerxes that he might rebuild Judah (Neh. 2:1-8). Daniel appealed to his commander not to be forced to defile himself with King Nebuchadnezzar's food and wine (Dan. 1:8-21). Paul appealed to a higher authority, Caesar, when Festus asked him if he would like to be tried in Jerusalem (Acts 25:6-12). Paul also appealed to a subordinate, Philemon, who was himself an authority to Paul's new convert Onesimus (the runaway slave) that he would accept him back and transfer his debt to Paul's own account (Philemon 10:19). Abigail appealed to David not to take his own vengeance on her foolish husband Nabal (1 Sam. 25:18-35). Abraham appealed to the Lord not to destroy Sodom should he find ten righteous inhabitants (Gen. 18:22-33). Judah appealed to the second most powerful man in all of Egypt (his yet unrevealed brother Joseph) to let Benjamin return to his father Jacob lest

Jacob die of a broken heart (Gen. 44: 18-34). Jethro appealed to Moses that he might delegate some of his judicial responsibility to other qualified men (Ex. 18:17-27). David appealed to King Saul to allow him to fight with Goliath (1 Sam. 17:31-37). David later appealed to Saul to stop pursuing (with the intent to kill) him (I Sam. 26:17-20). Bathsheba, with a bit of prompting from Nathan the prophet, appealed to King David to make Solomon king rather than Adonijah (1 Kings 1:11-27). Moses appealed to the Lord not to destroy His people as He intended (Ex. 32: 9-14). Hezekiah appealed to God to extend his life beyond what the Lord originally intended (2 Kings 20:3).

The Appeal and the Law of the House

Back in chapter two, I explained a concept called "The Law of the House." Parents, as you remember, are to develop a set of house rules specific to their home situation derived from their most sincere and diligent attendance upon the Scriptures. These rules fall into two distinct categories: *"Biblically Directed Rules"* which believing children will always be obligated to follow because they are directives commanded by God in Scripture (e.g. you may not lie, you may not steal, you may not take your own revenge, etc.) and *"Biblically Derived Rules"*, those which the parents develop based on biblical principles in order to facilitate their own obedience to the command:

"And, fathers, do not provoke your children to anger; but bring them up in the discipline and instruction of the Lord" (Eph. 6:4).

These house rules have been derived from Scripture by you as a parent and your children ordinarily would not be biblically obligated to obey them. An example of a biblically derived house rule would be: "Because the Bible says you must take care of your body (1 Cor. 6: 19-20), and it is vain to stay up late and rise early (Psalm 127:2), you may not stay up past 9:00 p.m. on weekdays, when you must get up the next morning at 6 a.m." However, because such rules have been established by parents, and not by God, children are commanded by Scripture to obey them, but only as long as they are lawfully under their parents authority.

Your child *may* appeal a biblically derived rule. ("Dad, there is a special program on television tonight at 9 p.m. that my teacher suggested we watch. May I break curfew to see it?") On the other hand, your child *may never* appeal a biblically directed rule. [22] ("Dad, is it okay if I steal a book from the library?")

The basis of an appeal is the presentation of new or additional information (preferably supported by a biblical desire and reasoning) that your child believes you as his parent have not considered in making a particular decision. Your child presents the new information along with its biblical justification / benefits (i.e. why the Lord might be pleased with a change of mind / decision) and without any further pressure allows you to reevaluate your decision. This process allows parents to change their mind without having to sacrifice parental authority. It also trains children to communicate desires biblically without resorting to disrespect, manipulation and other manifestations of sinful anger.

How to Make an Appeal

Biblical appeals, referred to in Scripture by such words as petitions, requests, and supplications, were made in different ways by many individuals depending on the personalities, positions and circumstances of the individuals involved. The following appeal process is one that has been devised for use by children with their parents. It is certainly not the only "right way" of making an appeal. I suggest it as a starting point from which parents may develop and fine tune a more personalized system for their children.

Step 1. **The instruction is properly [23] given by the parent.**
Step 2. **The instruction is properly acknowledged by the child.**
Step 3. **A request for an appeal is properly made by the child.**
Step 4. **The appeal is properly acknowledged by the parent.**
Step 5. **The appeal is made as additional information is presented to the parent by the child.**
Step 6. **The parent reconsiders his instruction in light of the new information and grants or denies the request.**

The Heart of Anger

Step 1. The instruction is given by the parent.

A key implication of Ephesians 6:4 is that parents will be giving commands to their children. These commands represent decisions that have (hopefully) been made within the framework of Scripture, but as mentioned above, are not necessarily in and of themselves, biblical mandates. Most parental decisions and instructions will be of the "Biblically Derived" variety. Although parents may not have a particular portion of Scripture in mind when giving instruction, the command should be consistent with the "instruction of the Lord" as found in the Bible with the ultimate aim of developing Christ-like character in the child.

Example: "I want you to be in bed by 9:00 PM tonight."

Step 2. The instruction is acknowledged by the child.

A child respectfully affirms that he both understands and intends to obey the instruction, thus placing himself in the best possible position to make an appeal. This step, in addition to demonstrating the attitudes of honor and obedience, tends to disarm parents from unnecessary defensiveness (pride), anger, and fear of being manipulated that might otherwise hinder objective consideration of the appeal. *"The wrath of a king (or an authority, i.e. parents) is as messengers of death, But a wise man will appease it" (Prov. 16:14).*

Example: "Dad, I understand that you would like me to be in bed by 9 p.m. tonight (and I intend to do so.)"

Step 3. A request for an appeal is made by the child.

By asking permission to make an appeal, (much like Esther did when she presented herself before Ahasuerus; Esther 5:1-3), your child further expresses humility, and submission to authority, communicating that it is your prerogative to grant or deny the request. This further prepares the parent's heart for objectively considering the appeal. A child's choice of wording is very important at this point. He is humbly requesting permission to make an appeal not questioning or challenging a parent's decision. Acceptable phrases include: "May I please appeal?", "Would you permit an appeal?",

The Appeal Process

"May I be allowed to appeal?", or "May I submit an appeal?"
   Example: "I have new information. May I make an appeal?"

Step 4. The appeal is acknowledged by the parent.

If you believe it necessary to hear the appeal, you may do so. Indeed, the parent would be a fool not to listen to an appeal that has been properly made. *"The wisdom from above is...reasonable (easy to be entreated. KJV)" (James 3:17).* If, however, the appeal has not been made correctly (Prov. 26:4), the child has begun to abuse the appeal process, or time will not allow an appeal at that moment, you may decline to hear it.

   Example: "Son, that is not the way you were taught to address your father. Perhaps if you choose a more gracious way to approach me, I will consider it later." (request denied)

   Example: "Yes, you may." (request granted)

Step 5. The appeal is made as "new information" is presented to the parent by the child.

This "new information" should include facts that your child believes you should consider; information that your child believes you did not consider in making the original decision. It *must be* information that was not known to you when you first considered the matter being appealed.

It was apparent to Esther that King Ahasuerus did not know that Esther was a Jew when he gave Mordecai permission to annihilate the Jews (Esther 2:20; 7:3,4). It was apparently new information to Philemon that Onesimus had become a Christian through Paul's influence and had begun to minister to him (Phil. 10-11).

Judah apparently perceived that it was new information to Joseph that Benjamin's father loved him so much that he feared for his life should Benjamin not return (Gen. 44:19-32).

It was apparently new information to King Saul that David had killed a wild beast with his own hands (1 Sam. 17:34-36).

New information includes such things as an expressed conflicting desire of another authority figure (i.e. parent, teacher, etc.), information that the parent would have no other way of finding out, and biblical arguments for considering another course of action which would better glorify God.

Example: "My teacher told us two days ago that a television special about the Civil War will be on tonight at 9 p.m. She suggested that if we were permitted to watch it, it would help prepare us for the lesson tomorrow. May I please stay up to watch the program?"

Step 6. The parent reconsiders his instruction in light of the new information and grants or denies the request.

By this time you can usually evaluate the additional data on their own merit (and in light of the Scriptures) without the distraction of typical concerns such as disrespect and manipulation. Should you grant the appeal, you can do so without being pressured into it and without compromising in any way your biblical authority. Should you deny the appeal you can explain your reasoning to your child without being distracted by the same problems. If you cannot think of a good (biblical) reason to deny the request, you might consider postponing the final verdict until you have thought it through more thoroughly.

Example: "Yes, you may watch the program after you have showered, brushed your teeth, and put on your pajamas so that you will be able to go to bed immediately after the special."

Example: "No, your mother and I made plans to do something else tonight that will require our not being distracted. Had you told one of us about the program when you first learned of it two days ago, we would have made other arrangements. I'm sorry, but I'll have to deny your request."

Example: (Postponement) "Your mother and I have made other plans tonight that will require our not being distracted. Why don't you prepare for bed so that your mother and I will have some time to discuss the matter between ourselves. When you've finished we will let you know what we've decided."

The following example further illustrates proper employment of the appeal process.

The Appeal Process

Step 1. The instruction is given by the parent.
"Go upstairs and clean your room."

Step 2. The instruction is acknowledged by the child.
"Yes, Ma'am! I realize that my room needs attention immediately..."

Step 3. A request for an appeal is made by the child.
"But, would you permit me to make an appeal?"

Step 4. The appeal is acknowledged by the parent.
"Go ahead."

Step 5. The appeal is made as additional data are presented to the parent by the child.
"Last night Dad asked me to wash his pick-up today. If I follow your instructions first and attend to my room, by the time I finish, it will be dark. Dad doesn't think I do a good job washing his car after the sun goes down because I can't see as well. Would it be all right if I washed his car first, then worked on my room?"

Step 6. The parent reconsiders his instruction in light of the new information.
"I've got a better idea! You may wash my car and Dad's car now. Then after supper I'll help you clean up your room."

Guidelines For Making an Appeal

Guideline 1. An appeal may only be made to the parent who is presently giving the instruction.
To do otherwise would be manipulative. It would also be disruptive of parental unity (Gen. 2:24) and contradictory to the principle of parental authority (Gal. 4:1,2).

One parent should not entertain appeals from a child who has been instructed by another parent unless it is impossible for the child to respond directly to the instructing parent. A child who attempts to do so should be sent immediately back to the instructing parent for consideration of the appeal (and possible consideration of disciplinary consequences for violating this guideline).

Guideline 2. An appeal will only be considered by the appropriate parent if the child's verbal and non-verbal communication reflect both submission to and respect for authority.

All appeals should be made using such words, tones of voice, and non-verbal communication (refer to the communication pie in chapter three) that shows parental respect and submission (Eph. 6:1,2). Thus, appeals attempted with manifestations of sinful anger, pouting, sulking, whining, sarcasms, etc., are not accepted. Rather, your child should be warned that he is violating biblical principles of communication and disciplined accordingly. In some cases, a trip to The Think Room would even be in order. In any event, the appeal should not be considered until your child has corrected inappropriate attitudes. When appealed to in a disrespectful or unsubmissive manner, you may respond as follows: "If you can put together a more respectful way to make your appeal, I may consider it. Until you do, I will have to deny your request. Any further disrespect will result in appropriate disciplinary consequences. Do you understand?"

Guideline 3. An appeal may only be made one time.

By multiple appeals (i.e. "But, Mom, pleeeeease!"; "Why?"; "Well, then can I...?") your child demonstrates an unwillingness to graciously accept a "no" answer from you and ultimately from the sovereign Lord Himself (Rom. 13:1,2; Col. 3:20; Eph. 6:1). If your child cannot persuade you to reconsider his position after one appeal, he is to conclude that it is apparently "God's will" (1 Pet. 2:13-15) for him to follow your instruction. Knowing that he only has "one chance" to approach you, should motivate him to give it his "best effort." That attempt may involve doing any appropriate research beforehand, working on (practicing if necessary) the development of the proper wording, tone of voice and non-verbal communication, and waiting for the best time (like Esther did) to make the request. Hastily made appeals often result in declines, whereas more thought-out appeals tend to be more successful.

Guideline 4. An appeal is to be considered a privilege that must be earned rather than an unalienable right.

The privilege of an appeal should come only to children who have faithfully demonstrated trustworthiness. Children whose decisions are characterized by wisdom earn the respect necessary to be entrusted to make an appeal. Children who characteristically make foolish choices are probably not trustworthy enough to make appeals in a proper manner (let alone with the proper motives). The Bible warns against placing confidence in unfaithful men (Prov. 12:19). Children who abuse the appeal process by making so many appeals that appealing becomes more of a pattern than obedience or who constantly violate any of the four guidelines should likely be suspended temporarily from appeal privileges.

Every Christian finds himself in subordinate positions at various times in his life. Many of these relationships are ordained by God, and submission by the subordinate to the superior, is required by Scripture. Christian wives are to be submissive to their own husbands (cf. 1 Peter 3:1). Church members are told, *"Obey your (church) leaders and submit to them" (Heb. 13:17)*. Christian citizens are commanded to *"be in subjection to the governing authorities" (Rom. 13:1)*, believing slaves (and by application— believing employees) are to *"be obedient to those who are their masters (and by analogy— employers) according to the flesh" (Eph. 6:5);* and as a general rule,— Christians are to *"be subject to one another in the fear of Christ" (Eph. 5:21)*.

Since the ability to make an effective appeal is crucial to any interpersonal relationship involving authority, training children how to appeal to their parents helps prepare them for lifelong success in such relationships. This character training also teaches them how to obey— *"Let your speech always be with grace, seasoned (as it were) with salt, so that you may know how you should respond to each person" (Col. 4:6)*.

Finally, there is something that is even more important than teaching children how to make a gracious appeal. That is teaching them how to graciously accept an appeal that has been denied. Perhaps you've never considered the fact that many of the prayers in the Bible are really appeals to God to change circumstances. Yet the attitude of the one praying is often "Not my will but Thine be done." I believe that one of the most vital elements of teaching children how to appeal is teaching them how to view a denial from their parents in much the same way as a "no" answer to prayer from God. They should learn to think, "If I cannot persuade my parents to change their mind after one well thought out, respectful appeal, then I must conclude that it is apparently not God's will for me to get what I want at this point in time. He is sovereignly working through my parents to conform me to the image of His Son. I will be thankful for this denied appeal and cooperate with His sanctifying work in my life."

A Good Investment

Perhaps you are saying, "I see how effective the tools explained in this book can be in training my child, but they are so time consuming. I'm not sure that I have the time to invest in training my child to overcome his anger problem."

Let me respond by saying *emphatically* that the resources described in this book *are* time consuming— especially at first. Yet in the long run, the time invested initially will compound into a much greater saving of time (not to mention other profits that have immense value for time and eternity) than would otherwise be spent on dealing with the consequences of a life that has not been trained in righteousness. Remember also, that God has given every one the same amount of time— 168 hours a week. If you are not able to fulfill all of your biblical responsibilities (not the least of which is child training for the Christian parent) within this framework, then either one of two things is askew: either you are wasting time or you have assumed some responsibility that God did not want you to assume. Perhaps you (and your spouse) should evaluate the degree to which you may be wasting time. Then re-evaluate the responsibilities you have assumed in light of the time it may take to fulfill the biblical responsibility of bringing your children up in the discipline and instruction of the Lord.

"It Didn't Work!"

Christian counselors regularly hear from discouraged counselees, "I tried it God's way and it didn't work." As a biblical counselor, however, I know that if a Christian makes such a claim, either one of two things is wrong: either the counselee did not really do it God's way, or he did not do it God's way long enough. The Christian may not have really done what the Bible says. Usually he has not done all that the Bible says do.

My response to them is usually this, "You say you've tried it God's way and it did not work? Would you please tell me exactly what you did when you did it God's way?"

"I did A, B, C, D, and E."

"Go on."

"I told you I did A, B, C, D, and E."

"Well, I thought you said you did it God's way."

"I did do it God's way. I did A, B, C, D, and E."

"But, what about F, G, H, I and J?"

"Oh! You mean F, G, H, I and J are God's way too?"

"Yes! Let me show you what the Scripture says. . ."

"Well, I guess even though I sincerely thought I was doing it God's way, I really hadn't done *everything* the Bible says I should do to solve the problem."

Doing the Right Things Long Enough

"You say you've tried it God's way and it didn't work. Would you please tell me exactly what you did?"

"Sure.— I did A, B, C, D, E, F, G, H, I, and J."

"You did A, B, C, D, E, F, G, H, I, and J and it didn't work?"

"That's right."

"Well, as far as I know that *is* God's way and it *should've* worked. How long did you try it?"

"Oh, about a week and a half."

"For you have need of endurance, so that after you have done the will of God, you may receive the promise" (Heb. 10:36 NKJV).

Remember it is usually not *while* you are doing, but *after* you have done the will of God, day in and day out for a period of time, that you will obtain the promise.

174

A Good Investment

Don't Give Up!

Jim and Linda didn't. Christian parent, do not lose heart in doing good, for in due time you shall reap if you do not grow weary (c.f. Gal. 6:9). Training children to overcome sinful anger is one of those good things that requires endurance.

The word endurance is mentioned four times in the first seven verses of Hebrews chapter twelve. This is the chapter in the Bible that addresses how a Christian should respond when the Lord disciplines him. It has much to say about child discipline, but speaks largely about the attitude of the child toward the parent during the disciplinary process. That attitude is one of anticipatory endurance rooted in the hope of growing increasingly more holy and righteous. If you expect your angry children to endure your discipline, having hope that such discipline will produce in them the character of Christ, how much more does your Heavenly Father expect you to endure, having the same hope as you train them to develop the meekness and humility of Christ? As you invest the time, effort, and thought necessary to utilize the biblical tools and resources explained in this book, remember that "all discipline for the moment seems not to be joyful, (neither for child nor the parent) but sorrowful, yet to those who have been trained by it, *afterwards* it yields the peaceful fruit of righteousness" (Heb. 12:11).

May God Richly Bless you as you apply His Word to your parenting.

Appendices

Appendix A

What Does It Mean to Forgive?

You are commanded to forgive,—

". . . just as God in Christ also has forgiven you" (Eph. 4:32).

What does that mean? God says,—

"I, even I, am the one who wipes out your transgressions for My own sake; And I will not remember your sins" and "I will forgive their iniquity, and their sin I will remember no more" (Isa. 43:25, Jer. 31:34).

So, does God have amnesia? Certainly not! God is omniscient (all knowing) and knew about your sins even before you committed them. When the Bible speaks of God forgetting our sins, it refers to the fact that when a person has truly been forgiven by God, He does not hold them against the forgiven sinner. He doesn't charge them to our account. Rather, God will charge them to the account of the Lord Jesus Christ, who died on the cross to pay the price of the penalty of guilty sinners like you and me. Christ's death was a substitution. He died to take the punishment for our sin so that we as saved individuals might be credited with His righteousness. When we truly believe the Gospel, God *promises* to not hold our sins against us. Instead, He imputes the perfect righteousness of His Son to our account. What is the Gospel (or good news)? The Gospel is simply this, if we repent and place our faith in what Christ has done by substituting himself for us on the cross and rising from the dead, God promises to forgive all of our sins and give us eternal life.

Forgiveness, therefore, is first and foremost a *promise*. As God promised not to hold the sins of repentant sinners against them, so we also must promise not to hold the sins of those we've forgiven against them. You may demonstrate this promise by not doing at least three things to the person you've forgiven. First, you may not bring up the forgiven offence to the forgive person so as to use it against him. Second, you may not discuss the forgiven offence with others. Finally, you may not dwell on the forgiven offence yourself but rather remind yourself that you have forgiven your offender, *"just as God in Christ also has forgiven you."*

For a thorough treatment of this subject see: *From Forgiven to Forgiving,* by Jay E. Adams, Amityville: Calvary Press. See a description and information on how to obtain this important work in the Recommended Reading section of this book beginning on page 203.

Appendix B

Guidelines for Training Young Children with the Various Resources Contained in this Book[24]

"When I was a child, I spoke as a child, I understood as a child, I thought as a child. . ." (1Cor. 13:11 NKJV).

Using the written materials in this book with children who are unable to read or write is possible when parents are able to reduce (or down size) the various journals from a "hard copy" to a verbal discussion. The following suggestions are provided to help such parents adapt the material to the needs of their younger children.

1. Use vocabulary that your child will understand. Rather than using the term "idolatrous desire" with my three year old daughter, I use the term "want to," ("Sophia, the reason you're angry is because you have a "want to" problem. You want to play with that toy more than you want to obey God.").

2. Use concrete illustrations rather than abstract ones in communicating with your child. Many of the truths your child must learn in order to overcome his problem with anger are abstract (forgiveness, gentleness, good desires and motives, overcoming evil with good, etc.) Using concrete, tangible examples, illustrations and applications of biblical concepts will make it easier for him to grasp both the nature of his own sinful behaviors, and their corresponding biblical alternatives.

3. Keep training times relatively short depending on your child's attention span. If more time is needed, schedule additional training sessions later that day or the next.

4. When attempting to draw out of your child (Prov. 20:5) what he is thinking when he becomes angry, you may want to introduce the process by saying something like, "Everyone gets angry sometimes, don't they?" You may inquire about the *circumstantial provocations* by saying, "Please tell me what happened when you became angry at your brother (or whatever piece of the circum-

stantial data you do have)." The child should then provide you with more of the circumstances that led to his becoming angry (the first question on the Conflict Journal, the Anger Journal and the Heart Journal).

5. When explaining the two sinful manifestations of sinful anger: ventilation (blowing up) and internalization (holding it in), you may find it helpful to use a visual demonstration.

For externalized anger, try this example with a soda can. Say to your child, "Let's pretend this can of soda is named Stan. Stan the can is mad because his mother yelled at him for getting up too late. He got really angry (shake the can) when his mother told him that he couldn't have his favorite breakfast. He got so angry that he exploded (pop the can and let the soda foam out)! This is just like the time you said that you got angry (repeat the child's example) at your brother and called him that ugly name. Do you remember what you did and said when you became angry? (Help the child remember if he cannot recall his behavior on his own.) Do you know what the Bible calls what you did when you became angry? (Explain the sinful manifestation using biblical terminology.) Let's see if we can come up with a few righteous ways that you could have responded to Mother so that the next time you'll be prepared to do what is right." (With your child's help, develop at least two biblical alternative responses to these circumstances.)

To illustrate internalized anger you may want to try the following. Form some Play-doh™ into a human like figure. Then, with the help of your child, make little knots out a different color of the Play-doh™, and place them on the neck and the stomach of the figure. Take the figures arms and legs and tie them in knots. Finally, splash some water on the face and hands of the figure to represent perspiration. As you finish this step, explain to your child, "This is Sally. Sally is very upset because her mother won't let her go out and play. If she complains, she knows that she will get a spanking, so she is sitting in her room getting madder and madder. Her throat and stomach feel like they are in knots. Her muscles are all knotted up and she is dripping with sweat. Sally is so angry that it is hard for her to even walk or talk or think right. This is just like the time you said that you got angry (repeat the child's example) when you wanted to stay up past your bedtime and Mommy told you that you couldn't. Do you remember what you did/said when you became angry? (Help the child remember if he cannot recall his behavior on his own.) Do you know what the Bible calls what you did when you became angry? (Explain the sinful manifestation using biblical terminology.) Can you think of one or two righteous ways that you could have responded to Mother so that the next time you'll be prepared to do what is right." (With your child's help, develop at least two biblical alternative responses to these circumstances.)

6. Time permitting, you may also want to consider role playing a few "unexpected reactions" to the biblical alternatives you have suggested. Remember what Paul says in Romans 12:17, "Never pay back evil for evil to anyone. Respect (plan ahead to do) what is right in the sight of all men." For example, you might say, "OK, you understand what to do the next time Jane tries to keep you from playing the game. But what if she hits you after you do that? Then how could you plan to overcome evil with good?"

7. After drawing out the outward manifestations of anger (the data contained in the Anger Journal: # 5 above), you may now proceed to collect data concerning the inward manifestations of anger (the material contained in the Heart Journal).

"How did that make you feel inside when you got angry? What did you say to yourself when you got angry? Do you know what God says about what you said to your self when you got angry at your mother and brother? (Diagnose the child's thoughts for him again using biblical terminology.) Now, we're almost done. You probably became angry because you had a bad case of the 'wannas'. There was probably something you wanted very much which you didn't think you were going to get. Can you remember what it was that you wanted when you got angry? (This should get you to the child's motive— lust, or sinful or inordinate desire). Can you tell me what is wrong with what you wanted? (Explain, again using biblical terminology.) Do you know what you should have wanted more than (or instead of) that?" (Provide the child with at least two biblical alternatives and relate them to specific Christlike character traits: i.e. love, tolerance, gentleness, forgiveness, etc.)

8. Young children sometimes have difficulty distinguishing between different feelings, expressing their own feelings, or recognizing different feelings in others. You can help your child in each of these areas by the use of "fill in the blank" statements. "When you were hitting your sister, if you felt angry, say 'I felt angry'" or "If when you realized that I was not listening to you, became sinfully angry and broke my vase because you felt rejected, say, 'I felt rejected when I thought that you weren't listening to me.'" Remember, the goal in this case, is not so much to chastise the child for his sinful expression of anger as it is to facilitate his identifying and expressing what is going on inside of his heart.

9. Where possible, cite examples where biblical characters talked to themselves (for better or for worse) during difficult situations. The Bible gives numerous examples of the specific (verbatim) things that people said in their hearts. These precise internal monologues can give tremendous insight into the character traits of each biblical character whose thoughts are exposed. Here is a smattering of the kinds of things men and women of the Bible said to themselves at crucial points in their lives.

Internal Monologues in Scripture

Biblical Character	Circumstances (Scripture Reference)	Internal Monologue (What was said in the heart)
Abraham	When he was told that Sarah would conceive (Gen. 17:17)	"Will a child be born to a man one hundred years old? And will Sarah, who is ninety years old, bear (a child)?"
Abraham	When he lied to Abimilech about Sarah (Gen. 20:11)	"...I thought, surely there is no fear of God in this place; and they will kill me on account of my wife."

Biblical Character	Circumstances (Scripture Reference)	Internal Monologue (What was said in the heart)
Esau	When he bore a grudge against Jacob (Gen. 27:41)	"The days of mourning for my father are near; then I will kill my brother Jacob."
Saul	When he enticed David into a trap with Merab (1 Sam. 18:17)	"My hand shall not be against him, but let the hand of the Philistines be against him."
Haman	When he presumed to know the king's mind (Esther 6:6)	"Whom would the king desire to honor more than me?"
The Wicked	When he attacked the helpless. When he renounced God (Ps. 10).	"I shall not be moved; Throughout all generations I shall not be in adversity." "Thou wilt not require it."
The Fool	When he "... has said in his heart..." (Ps. 14:1)	"There is no God." or (possibly) "No God!"
Satan Lucifer	When he said in his heart... (Isa. 14:12-13)	"I will ascend to heaven; I will raise my throne above the stars of God, And I will sit on the mount of assembly In the recesses of the north. I will ascend above the heights of the clouds; I will make myself like the Most High."

10. Consider using role-play or a reenactment of a biblical scene to help your child see that other Christians have faced similar temptations down through the ages and have been provided with a way of escape.

"No temptation has overtaken you but such as is common to man; and God is faithful, who will not allow you to be tempted beyond what you are able, but with the temptation will provide the way of escape also, that you may be able to endure it" (1 Cor. 10:13).

The Heart of Anger

Ask him, "What might Daniel have said to himself before and after he was thrown in the lion's den?" or "What might have gone through Paul's mind when he was thrown into prison?"

Appendix C
Idolatrous "Loves" in the Bible

Here is a partial list of the "loves" that the Bible speaks of as being wrong. After you have familiarized yourself with these, you may want to do your own Bible study of words such as delight, desire, lust, pleasure, want and will. Doing so will give you a greater appreciation for the frequency with which the Bible addresses "the intents (motives) of the heart" (Heb. 4:12).

Idolatrous "Love"	*Scripture Reference*

Love of money — 1 Timothy 6:10
For the love of money is a root of all sorts of evil, and some by longing for it have wandered away from the faith, and pierced themselves with many a pang.

Love of self — 2 Timothy 3:1-2
But realize this, that in the last days difficult times will come. For men will be lovers of self, . . .

Love of approval — John 12:43
For they loved the approval of men rather than the approval of God.

Love of control (power) — 3 John 9-10
I wrote something to the church; but Diotrephes, who loves to be first among them, does not accept what we say. For this reason, if I come, I will call attention to his deeds which he does, unjustly accusing us with wicked words; and not satisfied with this, neither does he himself receive the brethren, and he forbids those who desire (to do so), and puts (them) out of the church.

Love of pleasure — 2 Timothy 3:4
But realize this, that in the last days difficult times will come. For men will be lovers of self, lovers of money. . . , lovers of pleasure rather than lovers of God.

Love of food — Proverbs 21:17
He who loves pleasure (will become) a poor man; He who loves wine and oil will not become rich.

The Heart of Anger

Idolatrous "Love"	Scripture Reference

Love of sleep
Proverbs 20:13

Do not love sleep, lest you become poor.

Love of darkness
John 3:19

And this is the judgment, that the light is come into the world, and men loved the darkness rather than the light; for their deeds were evil.

Love of simplicity
Proverbs 1:22

How long, O naive ones, will you love simplicity? And scoffers delight themselves in scoffing, And fools hate knowledge?

Love of cursing
Psalm 109:17

He also loved cursing, so it came to him; And he did not delight in blessing, so it was far from him.

Love of evil and falsehood
Psalm 52:3

You love evil more than good, Falsehood more than speaking what is right. Selah.

Love of silver and abundance
Ecclesiastes 5:10

He who loves money will not be satisfied with money, nor he who loves abundance (with its) income.

Love of one's own life
John 12:25

He who loves his life loses it; and he who hates his life in this world shall keep it to life eternal.

Love of this present world
2 Timothy 4:10

For Demas, having loved this present world, has deserted me....

Love of the things in the world
1 John 2:15

Do not love the world, nor the things in the world. If anyone loves the world, the love of the Father is not in him.

Appendix E
Sample Journals and Worksheets

The worksheets on the following pages have been provided for you to photocopy for your personal use with your children. Try to use a copy machine that can enlarge these original documents to 8 1/2 by 11 inches, (enlarge to anywhere between 125% to 130% original size) that way you can keep the completed journals in a loose-leaf binder for future reference. Having such a notebook available in The Think Room for your children to review, may help them apply the biblical principles they've learned in the past to the current issues they are trying to resolve.

Anger Journal

1. What circumstances led to my becoming angry?
(What happened that provoked me to anger?)

_____

_____

_____

_____

_____

2. What did I say/do when I became angry?
(How did I respond to the circumstances?)

_____

_____

_____

_____

_____

3. What is the biblical evaluation of what I said/did when I became angry? (How does the Bible classify what I said/did when I became angry?)

_____

_____

_____

_____

_____

4. What should I have said/done when I became angry?
(How could I have responded biblically when I became angry?)

_____

_____

_____

_____

_____

Heart Journal

1. What happened to provoke me to anger?
(What were the circumstances that led to my becoming angry?)

_____
_____
_____
_____
_____

2. What did I say to myself (in my heart) when I became angry?
(What did I want, desire or long for when I became angry?)

_____
_____
_____
_____
_____

3. What does the Bible say about what I said to myself when I
became angry? (What does the Bible say about what I wanted?)

_____
_____
_____
_____
_____

4. What should I have said to myself when I became angry?
(What should I have wanted more than my own selfish and
idolatrous desire?)

_____
_____
_____
_____
_____

Conflict Journal

Circumstances surrounding the conflict:

_____

_____

_____

_____

_____

_____

Parent: _____

Child: _____

Parent: _____

Child: _____

Parent: _____

Child: _____

Parent: _____

Child: _____

Parent: _____

Child: _____

Parent: _____

Child: _____

Manipulation Worksheet

Circumstances Surrounding Manipulation:

_____

_____

_____

_____

_____

_____

Manipulative Remarks Made to Me:

_____

_____

_____

_____

_____

_____

My Response to the Manipulation:

_____

_____

_____

_____

_____

_____

Christlike (Biblical) Response to the Manipulation:

_____

_____

_____

_____

_____

_____

Appendix F
How Can I Be Saved?

How does a person experience the regenerating work of the Spirit of God? The Spirit of God indwells only those who, because of His grace, have put their faith in the substitutionary death of the Lord Jesus Christ. They are saved by grace through faith.

Each person, to be regenerated, must realize that his sin has separated him from God. God is both holy and just. His holiness disposes Him to hate sin. His justice requires Him to punish sin. The wages or punishment of sin is death. For God to overlook sin without requiring the appropriate punishment would violate His justice.

Try looking at it this way. Would you consider a judge to be just if, out of partiality to a convicted murderer, he sentenced him to only 30 days in jail rather than the minimum sentence required by law? Should such an unjust judge be allowed to sit on the bench? How about God? Would God, "the Judge of all the earth," be just not to punish sinners who transgress His law? Of course not! For God to let sinners off the hook without demanding that they pay at least the minimum penalty for their crimes would render Him unjust. The minimum sentence for sin according to the Bible is death. God must punish sin because His justice requires Him to do so.

On the other hand, God is loving and merciful. He *"is not willing that any should perish but that all should come to repentance" (2 Peter 3:9 NKJV).* So how can God forgive sinners in love and mercy, when His justice requires Him to punish them for their sins? The answer is to find a substitute! If God could find someone who was willing to pay the price for the penalty of sin and who did not have to die for his own sin, then He could punish the substitute in place of the sinner. But who is without sin? Only God. So God, in His love and mercy took upon Himself the form of a man in the person of Jesus Christ, lived a sinless life, and then died on the cross as a Substitute for sinners who were incapable of redeeming themselves. Then, after He was buried, He rose from the dead and in so doing demonstrated His power over death. This same resurrection power is available to those who truly believe this Gospel of God's grace. For those who believe, it is power not only over death, but also over sin— the very sin that enslaves us and that Christ died to save us from. You see, when a person becomes a Christian, the Holy Spirit indwells him giving him the power to change and to obey God that he did not have before he was converted. That is the essence of the Gospel, the Good News that should be proclaimed to everyone—especially to your children.

Appendix G
Correcting With A Central Focus on Redemption

The central focus of child-rearing is to bring children to a sober assessment of themselves as sinners. They must understand the mercy of God who offered Christ as a sacrifice for sinners. How is that accomplished? You must address the heart as the fountain of behavior. The cross of Christ must be the central focus of your child-rearing.

The focal point of your discipline and correction must be your children seeing their utter inability to do the things which God requires unless they know the help and strength of God. God's standard is correct behavior flowing from a heart that loves God and has the Glory of God as the sole purpose in life.

The alternative is to reduce the standard to what may be fairly expected of your child without the grace of God. The alternative is to give them a law they can keep. The alternative is a lesser standard that does not require grace and does not cast them on Christ, but rather on their own resources.

Dependence on their own resources moves them away from the cross. It moves them away from any self-assessment that would force them to conclude that they desperately need Jesus' forgiveness and power.

It is only in Christ that the child who has strayed and has experienced conviction of sin may find hope, forgiveness, salvation and power to live.

—Dr. Tedd Tripp

*This Appendix was excerpted and used by permission from **Shepherding A Child's Heart,** Tedd Tripp's essential book on parenting, produced and distributed by Calvary Press [18]. As the publisher of **The Heart of Anger** we strongly encourage you to purchase a copy of **Shepherding A Child's Heart** as it supplements the material presented in this book significantly.*

See a description of *Shepherding A Child's Heart* in the Recommended Reading section at the back of this book. To order your copy call Calvary Press toll-free at: 1 (800) 789-8175.

Endnotes

[1] Jim, Linda and Joshua are pseudonyms for a composite family taken from actual counseling cases from the Atlanta Biblical Counseling Center and the Christian Counseling Institute.

[2] There are 168 hours in every week. If I see Josh one hour each week, only to send him back into an environment that is making it easier for him to sin and more difficult for him to overcome his sinful habits (rather one that is making it more difficult for him to sin and easier for him to overcome his sinful habits), my one hour of *good influence* may be neutralized by the many hours of *bad influence* he is being exposed to in his own home. More importantly, time spent with Jim and Linda is necessary so that I may train *them* how to be Josh's counselors. God gave that responsibility to them, not to me (cf. Deut. 6:6-9, Eph. 6:4, Gal. 4:1-2).

[3] A person who continually gives himself over to the sin of drunkenness is classified by God as a drunkard (1 Cor. 6:10). One who continually gives himself over to folly is identified in scripture as a fool (Prov. 26:11). So it goes for those who continually lie, steal, fornicate. They shall be called liars, thieves, and fornicators. The complete list of characterological sins is too lengthy to cite here. Suffice it to say that "The evil deeds of a wicked man ensnare him; the cords of his sin hold him fast" Prov. 5:22 (NIV).

[4] Please notice that I said *"may defile"* not *"will defile"* (i.e. in a deterministic fashion). Christians may not knowingly allow themselves to be the "victims" of other men's sins. Christian family members should be taught to confront other family members who are sinning. Even young children (2 years old) can be taught (in principle) to follow the Lord's command in Matthew 18:15 ff.

[5] This increasing tendency to produce child-centered (man-

centered) homes can be traced to the widespread acceptance of humanistic philosophy into our culture over the past sixty years.

[6] H. Clay Trumbull, *Hints on Child Training*, pp 129-131. This work was out-of-print as of the publishing of this book but call Calvary Press for more information at 1 (800) 789-8175.

[7] In cases where one parent believes that the other parent's standard is clearly unrighteous the concerned parent should privately and gently discusss this with his or her spouse. Again, the appropriate Scriptures should be consulted and discussed. If no agreement can be made, parents should seek the counsel of others for the purpose of understanding and applying *all* relevant Scripture texts. Parents should continue conferring together until they can agree on a common set of standards that are based on God's Word. In the meanwhile, the parent who does not have the scruple should, in most cases, defer temporarily to the one who does (cf. Rom. 14 and 1 Cor. 8).

[8] Of course, clamming up can also hurt those at whom the silence is directed, and blowing up does also hurt those who explode in anger.

[9] Trumbull, pp. 1-2.

[10] "It is the glory of a man to overlook a transgression" (Proverbs 19:11). Parents should probably focus on correcting those violations that are habitual and be more willing to "overlook" those that occur more infrequently. "Love covers a multitude of sins." It is those sins that keep coming uncovered that must be especially targeted for correction.

[11] The Think Room is a form of discipline that last only so long as the child is unwilling to cooperate. It will be explained further in Chapter Eleven.

[12] Due to the location of my ears on my head some distortion exists here. Remember the shock when you first heard your voice tape-recorded?

[13] Adams, Jay E., A Theology of Christian Counseling , Grand Rapids: Zondervan Publishing House, pp. 114-115. Available through Calvary Press— call 1 (800) 789-8175.

Endnotes

14 Trumbull, pg. 14.

15 See Appendix C. for additional sinful "loves" identified in the Bible.

16 It is certainly not wrong for children to ask their parents "why". "Why" questions are illegitimate when they are used by the child with the intent to manipulate or falsely accuse his parents. As with so many things in life, what determines whether something is right or wrong is one's motive.

17 Zodiates, Spiros, *The Complete Word Study Dictionary,* Iowa Falls: World Bible Publishers, Inc., pg.222.

18 *pp. 145-146.* (In addition to publishing its own titles, Calvary Press is also engaged in book production and distribution for other publishers such as Shepherd Press, Wapwallopen, PA. For information on producing your Christian title through Calvary Press call 1 800 789-8175.)

19 As you read each of the suggested Christlike responses, remember that they must be read in a *tone of voice* that is consistent with the humility and meekness of Christ (Matt. 11:29; 2 Cor. 10:1). To read them with a haughty sarcastic inflection would be to miss the point of Chapter Five, that the tone of our voice often communicates more than our words themselves.

20 When the child has returned from the Think Room posessing a more repentant attitude, he should be more attentive. You will then be able to instruct him not only about the Heart Journal issues, but also about the "exceeding great and precious" scriptural promises that can deliver him from indwelling sin.

21 This chapter contains concepts that have been adapted and expanded from Growing Kids God's Way by Gary and Ann Marie Ezzo. Used by Permission.

22 They may, however, appeal your interpretation that a particular behavior violates a biblical principle.

23 "Properly" means "in a biblical manner." It means that the speaker's communication does not violate any biblical directive about communication. The speaker's words, tone of voice, and

non-verbal communication reflect grace, respect and the appropriate submission to authority. See Chapter Three for a more detailed review.

[24] The author thanks Maria Gangarossa for her expertise and assistance in the development of the material in this appendix.

Recommended Reading
Available from Calvary Press

The following pages contain descriptions of various other books which are published or distributed by Calvary Press and are being recommended for your reading because of their excellent content and value to God's people. Each one is a treasure in its own right. These pages, because of obvious space limitations, can by no means offer an adequate description of any one book or serve as an exhaustive listing of all the books we offer you. What you will find however, is a number of the books mentioned in *The Heart of Anger* as resources which the author found to be influential to him or particularly useful in the development of the material found in this book. There are also other books described which are very important to your parenting as well as important for your own growth in Christian doctrine and character. If you desire to obtain any of these books or would like to see a more extensive and current catalog of our offerings please call us toll-free at 1-800-247-6553. It is not enough for us to simply make these books available, what gives us the most joy and encouragement in our work is to get to know our book buyers and to hear how these books have influenced your life— so call or write us to let us know. Another important kind of feedback we appreciate from our customers is to find out about books which have been very beneficial to you but are now out-of-print. We strongly urge you to contact us so we may know about them and consider republishing them. In the past we have greatly appreciated having books brought to our attention this way. Well, we certainly hope you have found *The Heart of Anger* to be an enjoyable and spiritually beneficial book and one which you would seek to recommend to your friends, relatives, and congregation. Thank you again and May God Bless you!   —The Publisher

From Forgiven to Forgiving
Jay Adams

Calvary Press is honored to publish this desperately needed book on biblical forgiveness. Destined to become a classic work on this subject, it is a must for pastor, professional counselor and lay person alike. We've grown up learning many popular misconceptions about forgiveness from our parents, society and even our churches. The mission of Dr. Jay Adams is to challenge us through the scriptures *to understand the issues of forgiveness and to experience the power of forgiveness—as God intended.* This book has been greatly used by God and will continue to be instrumental in the saving of marriages, friendships, church memberships, and any relationship where issues of forgiveness have not been dealt with properly. A great book to be used for Sunday school or as a group study.

Thoughts for Young Men
J.C. Ryle

Do you have a young man in your family between the ages of ten and twenty five? Or perhaps you minister to youth (young men or women) in this age range. This book is simply one which these young people must read. The language is extremely readable and the message is as relevant to the young people of this current generation as ever because of the increasing moral and spiritual darkness of our day. Since Calvary Press' release of this influential work in 1991 well over 40,000 copies have been distributed worldwide. *Jerry Bridges* calls this book, "PURE SPIRITUAL GOLD". *John MacArthur* says: *"I heartily endorse this and strongly commend it to both Christian leaders and fathers, not to mention older and younger men alike."* Other commendations have come from *J.I. Packer, Iain Murray, Sinclair Ferguson, John Stott, Elisabeth Elliot, John Gerstner, James Montgomery Boice,* and many others. More importantly, thousands of young men have been touched deeply, often to tears, by reading this work. Although written to young men, this material is very suitable for young *women* as well.

From Religion to Christ
Peter Jeffery

Under the cover of a dark night, Nicodemus, a gray-haired Jewish Rabbi approached a much younger Jesus of Nazareth to inquire about matters which were deeply troubling to him. In this book, we are taken back to that intriguing conversation and are shown how the words spoken by Jesus on a hillside outside Jerusalem almost two millennia ago are essential to our salvation today. The author is deeply concerned that millions of people are just like Nicodemus was that night—religious, but still not redeemed by God. A careful and prayerful reading of this book can be used by God to open the eyes of many to finally see clearly that the religion they trust so much in is actually empty and vain, but that salvation can and will be found in Jesus Christ alone. One scholar has said regarding the issues covered in this book: *"To be ignorant of these matters, is to be on the broad way which leads to destruction."*

The Mission of
Calvary Press

The ministry of Calvary Press is firmly committed to publishing and distributing quality Christian literature relevant to the dire needs of the church and the world at the beginning of the 21st century. We unashamedly stand upon the foundation stones of the Reformation of the 16th century—Scripture alone, Faith alone, Grace alone, Christ alone, and God's Glory alone!

Our prayer for this ministry is found in two portions taken from the Psalms: "And let the beauty of the LORD our God be upon us, And establish the work of our hands for us; Yes, establish the work of our hands." (Psalm 90:17) & "Not unto us, O LORD, not unto us, but to Your name give glory." (Psalm 115:1).

Thoughts for Young Men
J.C. Ryle

Do you have a young man in your family between the ages of ten and twenty five? Or perhaps you minister to youth (young men or women) in this age range. This book is simply one which these young people must read. The language is extremely readable and the message is as relevant to the young people of this current generation as ever because of the increasing moral and spiritual darkness of our day. Since Calvary Press' release of this influential work in 1991 well over 40,000 copies have been distributed worldwide. *Jerry Bridges* calls this book, "PURE SPIRITUAL GOLD". *John MacArthur* says: *"I heartily endorse this and strongly commend it to both Christian leaders and fathers, not to mention older and younger men alike."* Other commendations have come from *J.I. Packer, Iain Murray, Sinclair Ferguson, John Stott, Elisabeth Elliot, John Gerstner, James Montgomery Boice,* and many others. More importantly, thousands of young men have been touched deeply, often to tears, by reading this work. Although written to young men, this material is very suitable for young *women* as well.

The Mission of Calvary Press

The ministry of Calvary Press is firmly committed to publishing and distributing quality Christian literature relevant to the dire needs of the church and the world at the close of the 20th century. We unashamedly stand upon the foundation stones of the Reformation of the 16th century— Scripture alone, Faith alone, Grace alone, Christ alone, and God's Glory alone!

Our prayer for this new ministry is found in two portions taken from the Psalms: "And let the beauty of the LORD our God be upon us, And establish the work of our hands for us; Yes, establish the work of our hands." (Psalm 90:17) & "Not unto us, O LORD, not unto us, but to Your name give glory." (Psalm 115:1).